We've Got Feelings Too

Presenting the Sentient Property Solution

by
Carolyn B. Matlack, JD

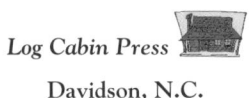

Log Cabin Press
Davidson, N.C.

Copyright © 2006 Carolyn B. Matlack, JD

All rights reserved. No part of this book may be reproduced or transmitted in any form or by any means, electronic or mechanical, including photocopying, recording, or by any information storage and retrieval system, without permission in writing from the publisher.

This book is a work of creative nonfiction. Although based in fact, some names and places have been changed to protect privacy. While legal principles and procedures have been simplified, every attempt has been made to make them recognizable enough to allow trained persons to identify and be able to work with them.

Published by Log Cabin Press
P.O. Box 2249
Davidson, N.C. 28036

Book orders: www.WeveGotFeelingsToo.com or www.animalfeelingsthebook.com

Publisher's Cataloging-in-Publication Data
Matlack, Carolyn B.

We've got feelings too : presenting the sentient property solution.
Davidson, N.C. : Log Cabin Press, 2006.

p. ; cm.
ISBN: 0-9776478-0-3
ISBN13: 978-0-9776478-0-4

1. Animal welfare-Moral and ethical aspects. 2. Animal welfare-Law and legislation. I. Title.

HV4708.M38 2006
179/.3-dc22   2006921795

Book production and coordination by Jenkins Group, Inc. • www.bookpublishing.com
Interior design by Debbie Sidman
Cover design by Melissa Lingle
Edited by Barbara K. Lawing, April Turner

Printed in the United States of America
10 09 08 07 06 • 5 4 3 2 1

ATTENTION CORPORATIONS, ORGANIZATIONS & SCHOOLS:
This book is available at quantity discounts with bulk purchases. For information, please contact Log Cabin Press at www.WeveGotFeelingsToo.com.

Dedication

To all nonhuman animals . . .
Those I am privileged to know,
Those I will come to know,
All the rest I will never know and . . .

To two human animals,
Mom and Dad
Sylvia Marie Lêcher Birckhead,
November 28, 1919 – August 21, 2003
Lewis Matlack Birckhead
July 3, 1919 –, and . . .

To you, the heroes and heroines of the future
who use sentient or feeling property to
modernize legal reality for animals.

Feelings

My life is full of meaning to me.
The life around me must be full of significance to itself.

And let us not forget that some of the more evolved animals show that they have feelings and are capable of impressive, sometimes amazing acts of fidelity and devotion.

The ethic of *Reverence for Life* prompts us to keep each other alert to what troubles us and to speak and act dauntlessly together in discharging the responsibility that we *feel*.

—*Albert Schweitzer*

Contents

	Foreword	ix
	Introduction	xiii
	In Tribute to Jolene	xvi
1	A Complicated Relationship	1
2	Moving On	7
3	Carpe Diem	15
4	Teddy's Case—Part One	19
5	Heroes & Heroines	29
6	The Visit	43
7	Spirit's Story	51
8	Research, Results and . . . Roaches?	63
9	Partners on the Path	67
10	How It Works	81
11	Teddy's Case—Part Two	83

CONTENTS

12	Expecting the Unexpected	101
13	A Modern *Lassie-Come-Home* Miracle	105
14	Closeness and Closure	109
15	Your Turn	113
	Epilogue	116

Foreword

It's a small world. I knew Jolene Marion back when she was an animal law attorney in NYC and consulted with her on several issues and cases, including the one involving Spirit. I was absolutely convinced that Spirit's case in the hands of Jolene would mark a precedent-changing direction for animal law.

Because I am a veterinarian and an attorney, Jolene and I shared a deep interest in the law's antiquated view of pets as property. It is true that she was a pioneer. It is heartening that now, many years after her passing an author is telling her story and blazing new trails in this highly important area of the law.

Because of my respect for Jolene, when Carolyn Matlack, JD first called me to discuss her interest in this subject and her efforts to write this book, I knew I wanted to be among the first to read it. I am flattered that she also asked me to draft a foreword to it.

As I read and learned of Jolene's story, Ms. Matlack's efforts to wrap some meaning around it, and the law's archaic view of animals, I became fascinated by her desire to "find the middle ground." I have taught veterinary and animal law to thousands of veterinary students since 1978, always espousing a point of view somewhere between that of the radical animal-rights activists and the overly conservative animal-rights activists. Over and over I have taught my students that the moral indignation for better treatment of animals that accompanies ethical arguments loses out to laws and court decisions. In other words, it is fine to make strong ethical arguments for better treatment of animals but the real way to win is with statutes, ordinances and appellate court precedents. The problem has been that legal precedents have fallen far behind society's view of pets as family members.

When I graduated from UCLA School of Law in 1973, I was certain that the law's primitive view that animals were property, worth nothing more than their market value, would quickly change. After all, in the early '70s courts in California and other states were rapidly opening the doors for lawsuits claiming damages for the negligent and intentional infliction of emotional distress. As a veterinary clinician practicing in California who saw firsthand how important pets were to our clients, I had no doubt that our patients had emotional value far in excess of their "market value." I would, and still do, ask my students: "What is the market value for a beloved 18-year old cat in renal failure?" The answer is, of course, "Nothing. In fact, owners will most likely save a lot of money if these aged family members were to die." However, as veterinarians we all knew and understood that the real answer to this query was that the real value of such a pet to a tightly bonded owner was, "Immense!"

In this great story that Ms. Matlack weaves, is the legal 'practicalism' of which I have always dreamed. I believe that this approach to changes in legal precedents can and will win out over the animal rights' "radicalism" that offends far too many people. Solutions to complex legal issues come one step at a time. There is no doubt that for progress in animal law to continue, society needs both the pragmatists and the radicals pursuing their views. Still, the steps toward a solution for our courts cannot and will not come in cataclysmic jumps; they can and will occur if sensitive and sensible attorneys, judges and juries seriously consider and apply Ms. Matlack's resolution.

I invite you to read, dream, and ultimately act upon the intriguing legal arguments Ms. Matlack has set forth in this unique book about animals and animal law. The legal arguments are challenging. Yet, the story is a great one, written in a manner that appeals to a broad audience. Best of all, the conclusion is on target, i.e., it is time lawyers and judges used the same legal precedents they have applied in a myriad of other cases to move animal law from the Dark Ages to the New Millennium.

—*Dr. James F. Wilson, DVM, JD*
Professor of Veterinary Medicine,
Author, Lawyer and Veterinary Management Consultant

Introduction

Animals are part of our family. Yet the law doesn't see them that way. Is there a solution?

I thought there must be and felt called to find one. The way toward making a big-picture difference seemed to lie in one of two directions, like being at a fork on a wooded trail. The left fork sign read 'Political Path' and the right fork was called 'Legal Lane.' Due to tendencies to assert my opinions regardless of the consequences, I knew choosing the Political Path would be useless. By default, that left Legal Lane and meant returning to school.

Applying to law schools in the middle of a busy corporate career filled with travel and deadlines seemed an enormous task—a second job in itself! What would admissions committees do with thirty-year-old grades? Did I have enough brain cells still alive to get a decent score on the dreaded LSAT entrance exam?

But law school was only the beginning. *We've Got Feelings Too: Presenting the Sentient Property Solution* weaves years of research and true events with personal life challenges into a creative nonfiction remedy that speaks not to lawyers, but to the animal lovers who will hire them.

Therefore '*Feelings*' is *not* written in 'legalese.' Everyone can understand the basis of how our current law sees animals. True animal cases, altered to protect privacy and sometimes for readability, tell the problem best.

Introduction

Headlines from one case in particular jumped out about a dog in an airplane: PET'S DEATH CLASSIFIED AS LOST BAGGAGE. I had to know more details. To find them, I thought I'd contact the lawyer who'd taken on the case. The telephone call was a shocker. Jolene R. Marion, Esq. had just died at age 53 the year before I started law school and the case was just now concluding!

That phone call was a pivotal moment which began a series of trips and face-to-face interviews with Jolene's sister, friends, former husband and visits to the places that were important to her and to her case. As time went on, I felt I came to know Jolene personally. She remains very much in my awareness today.

This sense of knowing her is one reason why I changed the timing of her death in *Feelings* so that we could "talk" as I imagined we would have—not only about her airline case, but personal hopes, dreams, solutions and her impending death. I hope our "dialogue" remains true to the details people shared with me during our visits.

Next, with the legal problem explained by Jolene's case and others I've included, I wanted to offer a solution that treats animals with greater compassion and respect. But so far there was none, especially not a practical one. Throwing blood on people wearing fur coats or banning animals altogether from medical experimentation just wasn't it. So what might work? That's why I'd gone to law school. So now what?

Hours led to years of research until I formatted a legal model to arrive at a next-higher step. Animals *are* legally our property but unlike the rest of our possessions, they have feelings! We know they feel pain, distress, love and joy. They are 'sentient' which is another word for 'feeling'. Animals are 'sentient or feeling property.' Sentient property. By actually using this practical new blueprint demonstrated herein by the fictional chapters about Teddy's Case, we can provide animals the fairness they deserve.

However experienced authors told me that what I wanted to do—combine the problem with the solution and fiction with nonfiction in one book—was impossible. And even if it could somehow be done, it would certainly take hundreds of pages or two or three books instead of one. "You would have to find a way to link the nonfiction problem with your untried and as yet fictional solution." Upon further thought, they continued, "The only link available is you. YOU must be the link. You have to put yourself in the book!"

I fought the idea for years. But all this study and research to improve animals' lives would do no good whatsoever unless people want to read about it, be able to understand some fairly complicated legal principles and perhaps be motivated to try them with a lawyer in court! If putting myself in *Feelings* somehow brought this about, then so be it.

I hope you find *We've Got Feelings Too: Presenting the Sentient Property Solution* is such a book—one you enjoy, learn something from and possibly act.

An editor told me that true art is cathartic. To think of my writing as a form of art felt odd, but she was right that it became cathartic. Being motivated to write *Feelings* has become a gift to myself. My life hasn't been the same since.

—*CB Matlack, Juris Doctor*

In Tribute

New York Daily News August 23, 1989

Jolene R. Marion, Esq.
April 21, 1941 – May 22, 1994

CHAPTER 1

A Complicated Relationship

My mother is coming.

This knowledge brought mixed feelings.

Our relationship had only gotten slightly less complicated as we aged. So while I was glad she was coming, I'd learned to expect trouble.

She laughed when I told her I quit my job. "That might not be the smartest thing you've ever done. In fact you've made some pretty iffy decisions before, but law school at fifty? Are you kidding? Can you study that well?"

In actuality, she didn't have a problem with law school. Leaving the security of a six-figure corporate job to study animal law, of all things, is what made me gossip material for her and her friends.

"Mom, I can't please you so I might as well do what I want." I might have had the nerve to say such a thing, but I didn't. I can't remember ever doing anything that elicited praise from this woman. In her eyes, whatever I did could have been just a bit better. Her most famous line was, "Well if that's the best you can do, then I guess we can't really expect anything more." I can still hear her saying that. Whether we were talking about playing the flute or trying to fix my marriage, I could always count on her to leave me feeling 'less than'.

When my brother called saying she was coming with the rest of the family to my graduation, it was my turn to laugh. I told him, "Oh, so now that she sees I'm graduating, I didn't drop out like she thought I might, she wants to be supportive."

He played the middle like he always does. "I think she's proud of you, Carolyn. Give her a chance to show it."

The thought of my mother saying she was proud of anything I did presented interesting possibilities. Dare I get excited? Had I not been so high on the idea, I would have seen what was coming. Instead I ignored what our history could have taught me. "It will be nice to see her," seemed simpler to say.

It's crazy. Even though my mother is at the root of my insecurity, she's also a person I greatly admire. She pony trekked in Sri Lanka and hiked the Greek Isles identifying her favorite flora and fauna. Her knowledge of botany is respected by some of the Who's Who of the plant world. Less than a month free of kidney cancer surgery, this woman is ready to travel from Michigan to Vermont for my law school graduation. She has strength and endurance any army general would envy.

I found myself drawing on her kind of guts to make it through that atrocious First Year that all thoroughly prepared law students had read about. Sometimes I know I'm turning into my mother as I get older. Sometimes this is a good thing.

A Complicated Relationship

Law school roared along like a grizzly bear or, perhaps a polar bear where we were. Vermont winters alone made me consider quitting. Winds slammed against the north side of the house and snow flew sideways in record feet, even for Vermont. When the white stuff got five feet or deeper, the roof had to be shoveled now—not tomorrow afternoon—or it would cave in from the weight of so much snow. Nor did Mother Nature wait for exams to be over either. She blew me into submission on more than one occasion.

North Carolina is a long way from South Royalton, Vermont in many different ways. Weather is just one. Driving in it was another. I had learned to zigzag the eight point eight hilly miles of snowy, gravel roads like an off-track road racer as I headed to the classroom finish line. At the wheel in that bitter minus-twenty-degree-air, I wanted to keep going straight to the airport and hop on the first plane heading south. Or anywhere warm.

But I stayed. I storm-proofed everything I owned, cut coupons, read every assigned book and every case at least three times. I went head-to-head with Professor Diggs every week until I understood every implication of each case we studied.

In the middle of all this change in my life, I started going through *the change* of life. So in addition to mountains of court cases to decipher, I labored under decreased memory capacity fragmented further by sweltering hot flashes. On the positive side, this extra 'heat' was one way to stay warm.

Every time I considered leaving, I thought about the reason I came in the first place. Peppy was my heart, my childhood friend and confidant. She was a beagle-cocker-mix my family adopted at the animal shelter. She was my first childhood friend. Together, we explored the local woods and traipsed the neighborhood looking for bird nests and ball games to join.

Whenever I felt like quitting, I thought about all the love she gave me no matter what my mood. I knew I had to show that her life, and all the others like her, legally means something valuable–priceless even. I resolved in my mind that Graduation Day was our first victory. "When I walk across that stage today, I know she'll be with me in spirit. Getting my mother's blessing will just be icing on the cake." That's what I what I told myself.

I should not have been thinking about my mother at all. You would think after half a century she wouldn't have as much power over me, but she did. She knew instinctively how to chase the sun out of the sky and let darkness rule the day.

To say classmates were happy about the festivities was an understatement. Bagpipes blared our arrival at the open-air tent on our quaint village green. The mood was nothing short of exuberant despite a cold spring wind whistling through our purple robes. We were just so relieved and glad to be among those who made it. We let our joy slip into giddiness. Continuous exchanges of 'Congratulations' 'Good Luck' 'See you at the reunion' buzzed through the air as if we had been the best of 'buds' throughout our common ordeal that was law school. One by one, Dean Newsome called our names.

"Richard D. Loudon, III" and the Loudon family cheered wildly. "Jane Lyston-Smith." Same thing. Her family led the cheering. With each name the applause became more and more enthusiastic. The professors seemed equally caught up in our euphoria, clapping and smiling along with us.

It was a small ceremony as graduations go. Our class only consisted of about one-hundred-twenty-five brave souls. But each family led the hurrahs for their graduate, in turn, as if shouting to thousands. "Roger Carl Mason." So much raw love and joy. You would have thought we were at a homecoming football game pep rally.

Until my name was called.

"Carolyn Birckhead Matlack."

Silence.

My family said nothing. They all just sat there. Instant, motionless, never-ending silence.

I was crushed but couldn't show it—not in front of all those people. I plastered a grimace-smile on my face, walked up those steps, across the stage, took my diploma from the (embarrassed?) smiling Dean, shook his hand, walked back down the stairs, crossed the isle and sat down in my chair.

Professors and classmates noticed. Even the breeze quit. My parents, brother and sister sat passively as if they were obliged to come to my graduation but cared nothing if I succeeded or failed as a law student or as a future lawyer.

One of my classmates tried to compensate by yelling, "Way to go!" His shout faded before he finished. More silence. The remaining names of the alphabet were announced, but the crowd's cheering fizzled to half-hearted polite claps.

After the ceremony my younger sister, Eleanor, rushed to my side. "I'm sorry." Being deaf, she usually signs but this time she used her voice. "Mother would not allow us to clap for you."

I carefully enunciated back. "She what?"

"She told us not to clap for you." Eleanor, teary-eyed, felt hurt too. I remembered the Christmas ornament she gave me before I started law school—a little female lawyer dressed in a cap and gown holding a scale of justice. She knew.

"Why?" I wondered. I guess I should have known, but I still never seemed to catch on ahead of time.

"She said we shouldn't act silly over you." Eleanor hugged me.

Mother strolled up smiling as if nothing happened. I wished I had the nerve to say, "Mom, if you weren't going to be happy for me, why did you come?" Eleanor had always done a much better job of getting out her hurt and anger. Why couldn't I?

She must've sensed what I was thinking. "I hope you're not upset because we didn't clap for you. You didn't expect us to carry on like everyone else did you." This was *not* a question.

"I expected this time you'd be supportive and not pounce on another opportunity to hurt my feelings." I wish I would've said that. Perhaps I was wrong, so I didn't. My expectations had once again landed me in hurt waters.

No one questioned her. To do so was unthinkable. It would mean taking one's life into one's own hands, which is exactly what I should have done.

She turned to my father. "Let's go shall we?" He cleared his throat and lowered his head. I lifted mine. "I have feelings mother, and they matter." Perhaps she heard me.

I couldn't tell.

CHAPTER 2

Moving On

"You can't keep letting your mother upset you. You let her run your life with those petty little comments." Jack and I get along better now that we've been divorced twenty-three years. We don't talk that often but when we do, I feel comfort. Talking to him is like throwing on an old sweat suit, curling up with a good book in front of a fire on a winter day.

"She has never liked me."

"She loves you—in her own way."

I could tell Jack was searching for a way to make me feel better. Emotions leftover from graduation still felt like my guts were hanging out of an aching open wound. "Yeah, but she doesn't like me."

"What's that got to do with it? Why do you care if she likes you?" He put on the kind of soft, slow voice adults use when trying to soothe a child. For an instant I thought maybe I should be offended. But I decided to go with my second thought, which was to listen to his gentle talk. "You're a great woman Carolyn. Most people couldn't survive the criticism you've put up with your whole life."

I closed my eyes to imagine what he looked like right at this moment. My insides warmed when I thought about the effort it took for this solid, six-foot-one, military lifer to be so tender. Even though we were talking through three thousand miles of phone wire, he seemed so near.

"Carolyn…"

I melted. All I could do was pour my heart out. "She's my mother. Everybody wants their mother to like who they are and be proud of them."

"But yours doesn't," he explained.

"Ouch." To hear him say it out loud hurt twenty times as much.

"And I should just get over it?" Jack's honesty could be brutal. I no longer had control over my voice.

"You have a right to feel hurt, but you don't have to stay that way."

It was still hard for me to allow myself sad feelings never mind let them show in front of other people. Somewhere I'd gotten the message that it was weak to cry and show your emotions. In fact, life would be simpler if they just didn't exist at all. Jack sensed me struggling.

"After all these years I've known you and dealt with your mother myself, you're right—I don't think she likes you. You lead an exciting life. You take chances. She told you she might never have had children if she had the choice. She's jealous of you." I pressed the phone against my face as tears fell down my cheeks.

"I'm fifty years old. I can't believe I'm crying over this still," I said through clenched teeth.

"It's okay, Carolyn." Still soft and sweet. For the life of me I cannot remember why I divorced this man.

I took a deep breath to get myself together. "How do I take chances? I am one of the most security-minded people I know." I needed him to tell me even the obvious answers.

"Quitting your job to go to law school, for one."

"I had to do that. I was bored silly at that job. I had done all I could do for that company." That was the truth. Leaving that job was more an act of self-preservation than bravery.

"I thought you liked your job. You said as long as you had a job working with animals you would be happy."

"That's what I thought at the time."

"What happened?"

"Animals, yes. But the time came to be more selective—to make a bigger difference for them."

"Huh?"

"Testing drugs on animals is not what I had in mind for the rest of my life, even if we did invent drugs to improve the lives of the animals themselves."

"Animal testing. You work doing tests on animals? I thought you worked with veterinarians."

Now I remember why we're not together anymore. Jack never did take my work seriously. Years ago when I told him that I could only feel fulfilled if I had a career working with animals he said, "You might as well get one of those jobs in a veterinary clinic. We're not making any money anyway." He didn't even look up from his newspaper.

Jack was in the Air Force during our marriage so, by association, I was too. Yes he was right; we didn't make a lot of money. 'Peanuts' doesn't even describe it. The allotted monthly living expenses for Air Force wives totaled one hundred dollars. But somehow his logic, 'When you're already near the bottom, you don't have far to fall' didn't feel very inspiring. Still, Jack was a great guy.

But the only way our marriage could've worked was if I wanted nothing more in life than to be his wife and have lots of kids. While that works for many women, I needed to make my own way. I wanted a career and it had to be with animals.

Plus, I was tired of moving. Being with Jack meant changing cities every time he received a promotion, which was every year or two. Relocating from pillar to post spelled disaster to a spouse's career. Back then, it was hard to imagine a compromise.

I think he blocked out much of what I said about my work. Truly wanting a career instead of children grew the gulf between us—come to think of it, so did his golf. "Jack, I haven't worked in a vet clinic since you and I were married."

"How the heck did you get into animal testing?"

"It's a long story." It wasn't just animal testing. There was more to it. I'd held various jobs; each one included working with animals but not all of them paid the bills. This one did. Anyway, I had explained it all to him before. I didn't have the energy to tell him again.

"What are you going to do now?"

"Animal law." I was ready to get off the phone at that point. Part of me couldn't believe after all these years he still thought I worked in a vet's office. He can be a great listener, but he must forget everything we say as soon as we hang up the phone.

"Pardon my ignorance, but what exactly does an animal law attorney do?" I could hear one of his sons bouncing a ball in the background, so I knew I only had half of his attention. Anything resembling sports always did that.

I cleared my throat. "Jack, are you listening?"

I could hear young voices chattering in the background. A door slammed and all was quiet. He was back. "Yeah, I'm listening. The kids are begging us to go camping this weekend."

By "us" he meant his second wife, Leslie. He remarried five years after we divorced and never looked back. She had no problem being the full-time wife and Mother he wanted. She moved with him anywhere keeping their household well organized, a feat considering they had four children. He couldn't convince me to have one. Motherhood was never to be my strong suit.

"Tell me about your animal rights."

"Animal welfare, not animal rights."

"What's the difference?"

Now I'm trying to remember how we ever got together even for the eight years we did. But his tone was sincere. I bit my tongue to hold back a groan. "There's a huge difference!" I knew my nerves were still raw. No need to take them out on him.

I remained under control. "I'm not an activist. I will be less effective in my work if I'm thought of as a zealot looking for fur coats to douse with blood-red paint." I had to add, "Although animals definitely deserve to keep their own coats," before continuing. "I want to change the law in a practical way. There are a lot of us out there now who feel the same way."

"What's wrong with the law? What law?"

"Our law. Our legal system sees animals as plain property." This was the whole reason I'd ended my life as I knew it and went to law school.

"You're talking about dogs and cats." A condescending tone replaced the previously loving and concerned voice.

"Yes. Companion animals. That would include cats and dogs."

"They're property? You mean like a house or a car?"

Here comes the argument in words I thought Jack would understand.

"Yes, but they are different. They have feelings. Throwing a puppy away like trash on the side of the road is not the same as tossing out a food wrapper. Both are bad, but the food wrapper isn't going to suffer."

Jack got quiet. I knew he understood what I was talking about. While I had grown up with Peppy, Jack loved his caramel-colored hound, Tippy. He knows first-hand that animals have feelings. Almost everyone does.

"So you're going to give animals the same legal rights as humans?"

I know that's what some people fear. If the law admits animals have feelings similar to ours then they think there will be a movement to grant human rights to animals. I have heard this concern *ad nauseam*—like the issue is black and white; either animals have human rights or they don't.

I wasn't talking to Jack anymore. I was practicing my argument. "I'm not challenging an animal's basic status as property. Rather the law should place animals in their own separate class of property called 'sentient property'."

"What does 'sentient' mean? How do you even say it?"

"Sen–tee–ent. It means 'feeling'."

"Animals should be property with feelings or feeling property. Sentient property. By creating this new legal category, courts will be able to recognize that animals feel pain, distress, love and joy. Sure there are animal cruelty statutes, although they're pretty weak. But there are so many other things that happen to animals, just as they do to us. Remember what happened to your old dog Tippy when that truck delivery guy ran him down in your own driveway and he died at the vet's? That had to be painful for both of you!" I knew the memory was still uncomfortable for Jack.

"Even if you'd sued the delivery truck company for Tippy's wrongful death and even if you'd won, the court may have awarded you money only equal to Tippy's market value. What was he worth? What do you think someone might pay you for a thirteen-year-old dog? Probably nothing. Zero dollars. Courts have no way to judge the value of living property any differently than they do a DVD player."

This is the subject I care most about in the world. I repeated for the thousandth time, "Pets are members of our family. Their worth to us, never mind to themselves, is greater than money. Their value increases, not decreases, with age."

Done. Again. Hopefully better that the last time I discussed it. Passion energizes me; at the same time, I felt worn out.

Jack sighed deeply. "Yea, I remember but I still don't get it." He was talking about more than just my new legal concept. After all these years we still didn't really know one another. I can accept that. "What do animal lawyers do? Can they make a decent living? Dogs don't vote or pay taxes you know."

I'd heard this before. It was a favorite line of my dad's. Jack still calls him every year on his birthday. Perhaps they'd consorted. Regardless, I wasn't sure how else to explain the importance to him. What words would he understand coming out of my mouth? I needed to be concise and straightforward.

"I am going to teach people in and out of court how we can treat animals with more compassion and respect. That's what I'm going to do."

He sighed again. "Good luck."

"It's going to take a lot more than luck, but thanks."

———

CHAPTER 3

Carpe Diem

Getting all of my stuff moved north *to* Vermont or, 'Verr´•mont' as some North Carolinians say, was a week-long project. Thankfully, two of my best friends had vacation time coming and helped me move up to Yankee Country.

Now moving back *out* of Vermont, I would be on my own.

Even though I bought a house here, I don't see staying in snow country any longer. Two months have passed since graduation and I have no prospects of a job. Besides, this area is lousy with lawyers—mostly Vermont grads trying make a living and remain in the area they'd grown to love. So I had to move again.

Most of my stuff shouldn't leave Vermont. I have lived in lots of places, from Nevada to New Jersey, and I can't see dragging fifty years of personal cargo all over the country with me any longer. Moreover, my checkbook had something in common with Vermont and its legendary temperatures—both were at record lows. If I believed my balance, the phrase 'available cash' was an oxymoron. I couldn't afford to move it all.

It would be nice to be independently wealthy. I was not. Asking my parents for financial help was never an option, especially now at my age. Besides, they'd paid for my undergrad years. Working harder was usually a solution and I was good at it.

I silently thanked my parents for the gift of teaching the value of hard work. As a kid, when I wanted more spending money than our standard dime-a-week allowance, I pulled dandelions.

I was paid one penny for every two weeds pulled with one major catch—I was only paid for the dandelions I managed to pull up with the entire foot-long root attached. Mom checked and counted them, too, before she paid me with *her* money.

Now, whatever money I had saved from my pharmaceutical career was about a month away from being gone. I knew when I left that job to get a law degree, I was walking away from something very valuable–financial security. Student loans couldn't cover everything. I had to figure out how to keep paying two mortgages for the house in North Carolina and the one I'd bought in Vermont and have enough money leftover for my dog and I to eat.

If I could introduce sentient or feeling property to the world, it would all be worth it. If I could keep that thought uppermost in my mind, the fears wouldn't be so terrifying.

I have learned when one door shuts, another opens. I just have to trust the timing. I heard a knock . . . literally.

"Carolyn, I have the perfect case for you." Jake, one of my fellow graduates, bounded through the front door with the enthusiasm of a young cocker spaniel. I felt better already.

"You're not going to believe this," he said darting through my living room like he had a severe case of ADHD. We had provided each other with much-needed support during the last couple of years using our own version of a five-minute pep talk. Besides, I knew Jake loved animals almost as much as I did. I could count on him for understanding in that regard too.

"Is Ed McMahon coming with the prize patrol?" Maybe that's what the universe had in store for me.

"Better. A buddy of mine from undergrad is arguing a case for a dog in a custody battle. The judge might consider where the dog wants to live–from the dog's point of view!"

"Are you serious?" For a moment I thought he might be playing a joke on me. But no, Jake wasn't the prankster type.

"Very. The judge might actually factor in the dog's feelings. This could be the precedent setter you've been looking for."

I had to sit down. My heart doubled its pace. I wanted to know more.

"What state?"

"Michigan." Jake grimaced. I could tell he had spent a winter or two in Michigan, another state where summer lasts from July 1st to July 5th. We'd both had enough of minus-twenty-degree temperatures to last us through our next three lifetimes.

"Don't tell me. Kalamazoo. Right?"

"How did you know?"

"Karma. What goes around comes around." It makes sense that I would have to return to Kalamazoo and settle a personal animal-related issue.

"I don't follow." Jake looked worried.

"I used to work in Kalamazoo."

"Doesn't sound like it was a very good experience."

"Nope. That's where my nightmares started." I stopped to catch my breath. Jake held his. I think he wondered if he'd done a good thing. "That won't stop me from considering work on your friend's case," I smiled. Jake relaxed.

"I knew you would. His name is Arthur Jackson. I took the liberty of calling and telling him about you." He finally sat down on the sleeper couch he'd used on more than one occasion after we'd studied into the night. I'd never seen him this animated.

"What did you say to him?" I was still more ready than excited.

"The truth. I told him that you are an idealist, strongly grounded in realism. I told him how you aced moot court so well you were offered a position on the school's competition team and how you got to see the same case argued for real at *THE* Supreme Court in Washington, D.C. I told him that you would've done a better job arguing the case than the guy who actually did it! But what really interested him was the fact that your arguments tend to be novel and creative yet practical. In a potentially precedent-setting case, that's what we need."

I had to admit, Jake was at right. I was far from the quickest. In fact I was a plodder. But I was, at least, thorough and prepared. Nor was I intimidated by judges. That routine was reserved for my mother. Even Professor Diggs appreciated that I knew the law and had the 'balls' to argue with him.

"Art wants to talk with you."

"He knows I'm not licensed?" I hadn't even taken the bar exam yet.

"He knows."

I thought I would have to be a practicing lawyer before an opportunity like this came up. I guess having a clear purpose can speed up the manifestation of one's dreams and goals. Mine had never been clearer.

"What's the matter? I thought you'd jump at this. C'mon. Carpe diem and all that." My silence confused him again.

"I'm ready. I'm just humbled and happy that this chance is coming so quickly."

CHAPTER 4

Teddy's Case—Part One

Arthur Jackson called me before I had a chance to call him. I had planned to call him at the start of the next business day, nine o'clock sharp. My phone rang at eight-thirty. It was Art. I liked him already.

"Ms. Matlack, Jake tells me that you're just the person I need to help me win this case." He sounded eager. I sensed he had been waiting for a case like this, too. His personal interest and dedication would translate into great work energy. I didn't want to

---

*Important Note: Teddy's Case as depicted in Chapters 4, 11, 12, and 13 is based on extensive legal research by the author about what *could* happen in a real court situation using sentient property to show animals greater compassion and respect. These four chapters are the 'blueprint' alluded to in the Introduction. Teddy's Case is but one example of sentient property's potential use. It is meant to be a compelling model and has not happened—yet.

align myself with someone who would give up or sell out halfway through the struggle.

Working in the corporate world teaches you that if you want to change anything, you have to have a lot of patience. Life teaches that. It also teaches that persistence pays. Trying to update animal law would probably take more effort than either of us had ever spent on one project before in our lives.

"I might be able to. Tell me about the case." I wanted to hear more before I committed. I also recognized the potential for this case to entangle me on a personal and emotional level too, creating both positive and negative reasons for working on it. But doesn't everything combine a yin and a yang to produce all that comes to be?

"There are thirty disabled kids living at Pine Haven Home for Delinquent and Disabled Boys. One of these boys is Ralph Sullivan. His parents, Mark and Laura Sullivan, just gave up custody of him."

I sat down at my desk. My house was pretty big for one person, so I had turned one of the three bedrooms into an office. I spent most of my day at the computer researching and writing. Two floor-to-ceiling windows allowed lots of sunny snow-light into the room. It was nothing for me to sit there for twelve hours straight. I could research any dilemma propped up in my cheery office.

"Because he's disabled or because he's delinquent?" My tri-colored collie, Moriah, put her front paw on my lap and pushed her lengthy nose under my hand. Her hopeful expression told me she was asking for a butt rub. She, too, liked the warm, natural light in the office. I started her rubdown, the phone crunched between my chin and shoulder.

"Both. These are mental disabilities that cause the boys to be unable to control their impulses." He talked faster than an auctioneer. I needed him to slow down.

"You're pretty wound up for eight-thirty in the morning," I said.

"I know. Some cases renew my hope in the law. This is one of them." Art inhaled like he was trying to calm himself. "I apologize. I don't mean to throw all of this information at you so fast."

"No, it's no problem. Believe me, it's not. I'm just glad to meet someone as eager for this challenge as I am." We both chuckled over our zeal, and then relaxed. "So what did Ralph do to get sent to the Home? How old is he?"

"Well, he's a big thirteen-year-old. He has been getting progressively worse with this impulse control thing. Two months ago, he physically assaulted his own father, Mark Sullivan, for no apparent reason."

"That's pretty scary. Is he locked up? Or can he come and go as he pleases?" Moriah whined. I'd stopped her doggie massage and had forgotten to fill her food bowl.

"He's restricted to the grounds. His parents didn't know what else they could do for him. They needed help. The short version of the Sullivan's saga is that they couldn't control him and no longer have custody. A shrink served as his guardian *ad litem*. This is where the case gets sticky."

I rose from my desk and headed toward the kitchen. Moriah turns into a relentless prodder when she wants her food. "I'm listening."

"Pine Haven proposed that Ralph be ordered to receive therapy."

"What kind of therapy?" That word 'therapy' gets thrown around a lot. Therapy to one person is goofing off to another.

"Impulse control therapy. But get this—Pine Haven wants the family dog ordered to stay with Ralph at the Home as a therapy dog. And guess what kind of dog?" Arthur paused, waiting for me to guess but he couldn't wait and continued, "A collie—an old boy at that!" Jake had apparently given him a lot of details about me, including Moriah.

Triumphant silence followed, as if this fact alone would clinch my acceptance of the case.

"Does Ralph want the dog? By the way, what's his name?"

"Teddy. Ted for short. And, yup, Ralph wants him. At least so says Pine Haven. Of course Ralph can't speak for himself. Pine Haven hired a child behavior expert who made the determination that Ralph wants the dog. The court used a guardian *ad litem* to represent Ralph using the Doctrine of Substituted Judgment to interpret his needs and wants."

"Okay." Moriah moseyed to her bowl as soon as she heard the dog food bag open. I quickly reviewed in my mind what I knew about the Doctrine of Substituted Judgment. It was an old and well-established legal doctrine that could be used in any situation where someone could not speak for himself or herself and therefore another person's judgment had to be substituted; perhaps the 'someone' was a minor child or an adult with Alzheimer's disease or an accident victim in a coma. The Doctrine would be well known in any court, so it would be perfect. But all the cases have been about human beings, not dogs. Could we get a judge to use it for a *dog*? I had an idea, but I knew Art wasn't finished.

"Here's the rub. The parents want to keep the dog. They say Teddy has lived with them for years and further, that Teddy *wants* to stay with them. They got an expert to back them up. A Dr. Foster, a psychiatrist, argues that the Sullivans have been through enough emotional trauma with their son. In her professional opinion, Teddy should stay with the family he has known all of his life. While Dr. Foster does not claim to be an animal behavior expert, she has gone on record stating that Teddy's behavior and demeanor indicate that he is happy where he is. He would rather stay with the Sullivans than with the kids at the Home. The Sullivans are prepared to hire animal behavior experts if necessary." Art spoke calmly and steadily now. I could tell he had slipped into his 'zone', like an athlete into his game.

I was ready to be on his team.

"Plus one would think the dog would be in some degree of danger living in a strange place with young troubled boys who may not always be kind to him," I added.

"Yes, that was offered as another reason Teddy should stay with the Sullivans. Mark and Laura are not going to hand Teddy over to the Home without a fight. They firmly believe Teddy would be in danger due to the boys' unpredictable behavior. He also exhibits stressful behavior at the Home. And get this. Teddy has already escaped from Pine Haven twice during scheduled visits! He found his own way back thirty-six miles to the Sullivan home. Does this sound to you like a story we grew up with?"

"Wow." The parallel to the much loved *Lassie Come Home* was remarkable—collie and all.

"So Pine Haven can get another dog to use for therapy." Moriah was nosing through her favorite chicken-and-rice kibble, so I headed back to my desk.

"You would think that might be logical, but no. Pine Haven hired an attorney, Michael J. Edison, to force the Sullivans to permanently give him up. The Home claims that it is essential for Ralph and the rest of the boys to keep him because Teddy improves the boys' social skills and keeps them calmer. Evidently some kids made remarkable progress when a former pet lived there. They make the point that this dog was used for therapy for years before dying of old age."

"But if Teddy belongs to Ralph's parents…" This didn't sound like a hard case to me.

"Teddy's registration papers state that Ralph is his legal owner."

So that's the rub.

"That's why Pine Haven thinks they will win this case." Things were becoming complicated.

"He's an exceptional dog. I met him. The Sullivans maintain Ted has clearly demonstrated his preference to remain in their home by a number of behaviors not the least of which is his running away. Ted *wants* to live with them. They say they would be willing to take Ted to Pine Haven for visits—supervised visitations only—but they are *not* going to

Teddy, aka 'Ted'

give the old guy up." I could tell by Arthur's tone of voice that he already loved this elderly collie.

"So they hired you to get Teddy back for them?"

"No. They hired their family attorney, Katherine Anderson, to represent their interests and petitioned the court for legal representation for Teddy himself, with costs assigned of course to the losing party."

"That's where you come in?" He didn't represent the family or the Home. He represented Teddy. Now I knew why he was so excited.

"Exactly. To support their position that what Ted wants is important, they have hired me because I got some attention last year for settling the Long case." Arthur relayed that last piece of information as if it was of little consequence, but I'd heard of the famous pet custody case and knew getting it 'settled' required skilled lawyering on Arthur's part.

"So you are to be Teddy's legal advocate," I confirmed.

"That's right. It will be my job to persuade Judge Lewis to allow the court to consider what Teddy himself wants and needs. Now here's where you come in."

"I think I know where you're going with this."

"Where?"

"You need me to help you find an argument that can be narrow enough to help Teddy specifically, yet broad enough to work for other animals too. Obviously, whatever this judge decides could be used in other animal cases across the country."

It was true. The implications of Teddy's case could be huge. Setting this kind of precedent where a judge viewed an animal as feeling property would have a real impact on animal law and animals.

"You sound like you see my strategy, Carolyn. You're right. I need detailed analyses of cases where an animal's emotions were factored into the judge's decision." I could hear Art's passion as he continued.

"Judge Lewis may be open to considering Teddy's feelings, but finding persuasive case precedent will be tough. Ralph owns Ted, end of story, unless we show other cases like his where an animal's feelings were considered in the case."

Moriah was back doing her best to be a lap dog again. She was the runt of her litter so she could almost fit. I bent over to give her small self a big hug, dropping the phone to the floor. "Sorry Arthur," I said picking it up and putting it back in the cook of my neck.

"I can research cases, no problem. But you know how outdated they can be. What we need is a logical way for judges to apply these archaic cases to modern problems." I was not about to let Teddy's case become fodder for late night television jokes if I could help it, even though the horse-and-buggy cases still on the books did make case decisions sound ludicrous at times.

"Go ahead. My turn to listen." Art lapsed into an expectant silence.

"Think of the big picture," I began. "As we speak, judges in courts across the country are hearing animal cases. They know the public wants fairer justice. Put yourself in their position. It's hard trying to write reasonable opinions using cases that were applicable a century ago. They have animals too, including Judge Lewis I bet. We can show him how to succeed without making him look foolish." I stopped. I wanted to see if Arthur agreed with my assessment so far.

"Of course. They don't want to be overturned by a higher court. That's a 'no, no' on their job evaluation record." Arthur resumed his silence, so I continued.

"That's precisely why we need to give him a new way to look at old existing doctrines and cases—just tweak them a little bit. Make the jump to the modern age as easy as possible."

Now I felt I was hitting my own groove. "We both know animals are currently classified as our property. Whether we call ourselves 'owners', 'keepers', 'guardians', or purple people eaters, animals are going to remain our property in the foreseeable future. Right?" I didn't wait to see if Arthur agreed.

"We also both know that animals are different from other property like a chair or a piece of luggage. We know they have feelings. I propose that animals have their own special property classification called 'sentient property'. *Black's Law Dictionary* already defines over thirty kinds of property. How revolutionary can it be to add another?" The phone line was silent. Arthur was using one of those annoying cell phones that often cut off in the middle of a conversation. "Arthur, are you there?"

"Yes, I'm here. I'm trying to keep up with you."

My turn to slow down. "Part of Judge Lewis placing Teddy in this classification would mean that we, or a court appointed guardian *ad litem*, would be allowed to use the Doctrine of Substituted Judgment to determine his best interests." I sensed I may have just lost Art entirely.

"Think about it. 'Sentient' means 'feeling'. Animals have feelings. Except for wild animals, animals are property. In Europe, animals are called 'sentient beings'. Blend the two together and you have 'sentient property'; a new legal phrase with both domestic and international implications for animal law. Sentient property is a more accurate, fair category for animals. It expresses our respect for them and our acknowledgment of their value as living, feeling beings." Even most lawyers know nothing about animal law. Art was an exception.

"Ralph was appointed a guardian *ad litem*…"

I broke in, "Because Ralph could neither competently nor legally speak for himself. Well, neither can Teddy. That's why you will be hired." I stopped. I have a bad habit of finishing people's sentences. "Sorry. What were you going to say?"

"That's okay. I think we are headed in the same direction. Go on."

"Thanks, Art. Since Ralph's case used a guardian *ad litem*, I think we would improve our chances of winning this case if you were officially appointed Teddy's G.A.L.—his guardian *ad litem*. That will create a clearer association between the two cases."

"So I can show how the Doctrine of Substituted Judgment can be used to determine the interests of an animal, Teddy, just like it was for Ralph," Art verified.

"You got it." He was a quick study.

"As an official guardian *ad litem*, I can explain to the court the need to classify animals as sentient or feeling property to distinguish them from cars or luggage or other kinds of property. Some cases have already *tried* to find a way to do that," he mused. "Then I'll show Judge Lewis how this new legal animal category can be partnered with the Doctrine to determine the interests of an animal and to produce a fairer outcome of our custody dispute."

We both took a breath. Art was really good.

"This will be the first case like this in the country. If we're successful, there's our sweet precedent," I chimed in.

I knew Art was using our pause to look for holes in my argument so I shut up.

"That's brilliant. How did you come up with it? You've only been out of law school for what? Two months?"

"Yeah, but before school I worked for years in universities, laboratories and corporations that develop products for animals or use them for research. I know what hurdles companies must jump to get products to market. I know what animals go through, too, and I know how callously some people treat them." I, too, took a deep breath.

"Arthur, I went to law school for the sole purpose of helping animals. That might make me atypical, or even just plain weird, but one of the best things about being older is that what other people think doesn't matter as much as it did when I was younger." I stopped to see what saying that to him felt like. Did I feel older? Yes, but freer!

"The emotional attachment between people and their pets can't be ignored forever; neither can we continue to legally pretend our animals are living beings without feelings. When is the last time your couch greeted you wildly at the door, as if you were a returning god?

I know we are ready to modernize animal law. Animals are too important to most of us not to. Team Teddy can do it."

"Right on." I could hear Arthur's conviction that we could succeed.

I summed up. "Our concern for animals has been growing for years. Especially since around the year 2000, the pressure to do something has intensified. Now it's beginning to erupt. There has never been a better time to set this new precedent!" As an afterthought I added, "If we are successful, I probably won't even take the darn bar."

"That would be a shame. We need prepared thinkers like you in the courtroom."

"Thanks Art. Nice of you to say that. I'll start gathering cases."

Art and I had connected. We were as determined to succeed as any two people could be.

I'm glad we couldn't see what lay ahead….

CHAPTER 5

Heroes & Heroines

Anyone that needs to make a lot of money should not go into animal law. It's just not there. Art offered me five hundred dollars a week to research cases. I would have done it for free if I could. I accepted his money because I needed it. I knew when I turned down this path, that my days of financial security may be gone forever. Knowing your purpose in life makes hardship easier to bear. My purpose was to introduce sentient or feeling property and let the results go. I knew whatever the outcome, I had done my part. It was the right thing to do.

I hadn't arrived at this decision easily. Sometimes figuring out the 'next right thing' can be tricky. I used to think it meant doing what someone else told me to or doing what the rules said to do. I'd changed. Now I knew I was getting to the core of what I was really supposed to do.

Circumstances and incidents began falling into place, though not as *soon* as I'd prefer. For example, a quiet, mature couple rented my North Carolina home. Income at last. I began a *Miracles & Demonstrations Journal*. Every page lists an event that was beyond my power to create. Each one seemed proof that I was doing the right thing.

For hours, then days and weeks, I scoured legal sources like Westlaw for cases relevant to Teddy's. One of the issues had to involve an animal's feelings or emotions. Further, I needed to find any laws, ordinances or statutes that already contained language where the phrase sentient or feeling property might fit.

I found recent animal cases that still used legal principles from long ago. We're talking nineteenth century here—truly horse-and-buggy era. One headline grabbed my attention:

1891 Opinion Bars Owner's Mental Distress Over A Dog

A Texas court recently ruled that a more than 100-year-old decision prevents Sara from recovering damages for emotional distress she suffered when her dog, Leo, escaped from a groomer and was run over and killed by a car. The Court, using *over a century old court case ruling*, said dogs are classified as personal property. Owners can only recover damages based on the price or market value of the dog.

Some of the cases were more encouraging.

A judge in Maryland allowed a lawyer's clever use of a legal fiction to argue on behalf of Nala, a German shepherd, and her disabled owner, Gretel. A legal fiction is simply an assumption that something is legally true even though it may be untrue. For example, a corporation is considered a person, an artificial being, so it can act legally as a single entity

Leo and Sara in happier times.

in a court of law. Using legal fiction is a way to call a spade a heart even though it's really a spade. Talk about legal mumbo jumbo!

I wondered how legal fiction was used in Nala's case. It became clear as I read the facts.

Gretel was a fifty-year-old woman who suffered from cerebral palsy. The cerebral palsy affected both of her legs and her right hand. She was totally and permanently disabled and required crutches to ambulate.

Gretel functioned with the help of two service dogs specially trained and constantly on duty to open doors with their mouths or brace them open for her with their bodies. They retrieved items she dropped.

On May 24, 1992, Alex, an eight-year-old neighbor, was walking Nala around their apartment complex in Adlersville, Maryland. A group of teenagers surrounded Alex and Nala and threatened them with rocks the size of softballs. One of them struck Nala on her side. Terrified, Alex and Nala raced back to Gretel's home.

Gretel prosecuted two of the juveniles who were found guilty of animal cruelty.

However Nala was left permanently emotionally scarred. Though her physical injuries healed quickly, she had been badly frightened and no longer had the same trusting personality. Gretel could no longer rely on Nala for help.

And Nala had become aggressive toward people who resembled her attackers. Her trainer said Nala needed to be desensitized at a cost of three to five thousand dollars. An alternative would be to replace her with another trained dog, at an approximate cost of twenty-five thousand dollars!

The Maryland Violent Crimes Compensation Commission concluded that the *Criminal Injuries Compensation Act* did *not* permit an award to Gretel for injury to her service dog. The victim had to be a *person*, not a dog. The Act defined a victim in part as a person who suffers personal, physical or psychological injury or death as a result of a crime." The Commission found that the victim of the crime was not Gretel, but 'the dog'; therefore there was no injury and thus no money to compensate Gretel.

Here's where the case got *really* interesting.

Gretel's lawyer convinced a judge that Nala was really a kind of 'person'. She argued that, yes, Gretel herself was indeed the victim of the crime; the loss of Nala's services could rightly be compared to damage to a prosthetic limb, since Nala served as a physical extension of Gretel—as her right arm metaphorically speaking. Therefore, Nala was actually part of Gretel's person. The judge agreed. He thought that in view of the function of the dog as a veritable extension of Gretel's own body, an injury to the dog is equivalent to an injury to Gretel. Gretel got her money. Nala got to retire.

While I admired this creative lawyering, no argument was offered about Nala's *own* pain and suffering or emotional distress.

Moriah resumed her position curled across my toes. I searched on for cases for another hour until my eyes began to rebel against me. Those annoying black floaters swirled across my vision. I contemplated taking a break. But then, spots or not, an interesting description of a dog named Boomer popped up on my computer screen.

"Boomer was a medium-sized spaniel-Labrador-something mix.

A jumbo head suggested St. Bernard or perhaps Newfoundland lineage. His curly, baking-chocolate-colored hair was soft to the touch. He was a roughhousing, playful dog with a golden soul."

Somebody loved this dog. I settled back into my chair as far as my vision permitted, to read more.

"Boomer's owner, Janice Finley, was 'special'. She was twelve and had a bilateral congenital hearing loss."

I had to stop right there. My sister Eleanor, having been deaf since birth as far as anyone could tell, would like this one. I hoped this wasn't another story about street-tough kids attacking a helpless child. My sister and I had lived through that when we were kids. Because of our experiences, I developed a lifelong concern for the underdog–human or animal. I'll never forget one childhood incident involving my sister.

Eleanor was often an easy target for mischief. Other kids teased her, especially for the way she talked. Perhaps they thought that because she couldn't hear, she was unaware of their taunts. She knew, and it hurt her feelings every time.

One day on the way home from the city swimming pool, an oversized bully named John, circled Eleanor. He swatted at her hair to amuse his friends with her low, throaty screeches. Eleanor tried to get away but he stopped her.

By the time I walked up, Eleanor was in tears. There were at least fifteen kids with more gathering. As a scrawny ten-year-old, I didn't say a word. The other kids were laughing, nervously I noticed, as I scoped out the situation.

John was the center of attention. To further impress his growing crowd, he picked up a stick and poked at her around her head and shoulders. As her hair became increasingly messy and tangled, Eleanor wailed in the deep tonal voice that Mom worked hard with her to lighten her pitch.

"Leave me alone," she blubbered in her deep monotone, her face red from crying.

The kids just stood there. John mocked her speech, "Leave me alone. Leave me alone." Too fast for me to stop him, he slung a rock hitting her in the back of her head. "Smack!" I will never forget that sound. Eleanor screamed. Blood gushed.

I snapped. I felt like superwoman—super stong and invincible.

I wrapped my swim towel around her head, grabbed John and crashed him to the ground. I beat him until my hands hurt. These weren't little patty cake licks, either. I've always had more than my fair share of physical strength at my disposal. After the first punch landed with a 'whap' on John's right eye, the other kids scattered.

When I finally finished pounding John's face, I looked up at Eleanor. The towel was dark red. Her face was stricken with fear. She'd seen me fight before, but never like this. John lay motionless on the ground. I knew he wasn't dead.

Later that night we learned that 'John the Jerk' would be partially blind. My ten-year-old mind thought for sure I would go to jail, but I didn't even get grounded. No one was prepared to punish me for protecting my deaf little sister. Even my mother let the incident go without a strong reprimand.

The episode was practice for later when I'd twice more do the same thing to protect an animal, one of them a Seeing Eye dog. Looking back, I'm not proud of this behavior but, honestly, I have no regrets.

It turns out Janice, despite her deafness, played the protector role in her family.

"On November 23, 1986, thirteen-year-old Janice and her mother, Joyce, were eating chicken enchiladas in a Santa Fe, New Mexico grill. They'd left Boomer at home gnawing a chew bone in the kitchen. After dinner and grocery shopping, they drove home.

Janice smelled the smoke first. She raced to the front door and flung it open. Black smoke knocked her to her knees coughing. 'Boomer, Boomer', was the last thing her mother heard as her only child disappeared into the smoky front hall. Joyce ran to the neighbors to call Santa Fe Fire & Rescue.

When Joyce returned, she knew instantly that her daughter would not come out before she found their Boomer. The dog was specially trained to help Janice with daily tasks, such as alerting her to a ringing telephone or a knock at the door. But Boomer had become more than an assistance dog. Being deaf can be especially lonely. Boomer was her emotional support, too. Fearing for her daughter's life, Joyce chased after her.

Boomer perished. Janice suffered third-degree burns. Joyce also suffered burns, a broken hip and shoulder. Their home was a pile of cinders.

Joyce missed five months of work as assistant librarian at the Santa Fe Regional Library. Janice's skin grafts took longer to heal than her mother's broken bones. Losing Boomer was most traumatic of all.

The cause of the fire was later determined to be a faulty switch in their coffee maker.

The Finley's sued both the coffee pot manufacturer and the switch company. They sought damages for their injuries, loss of property and emotional distress damages caused by Boomer's death.

There is a provision in New Mexico law that allows people who enter a burning building to save a *family member or another human being* to collect damages if they are injured. But Janice ran in to rescue her *dog*.

The question in their case asked, "Were Janice Finley's actions to rescue her hearing dog reasonable under the circumstances?" And, "Did Joyce Finley act reasonably in trying to rescue her daughter?"

Throughout the case, Boomer was never referred to by name. He was always referred to as 'the dog'. This depersonalizes the case. He is no longer a cherished member of the family, but merely a dog—a replaceable piece of property. We are less likely to feel the plight of the victim if the victim is 'the dog' instead of 'Boomer' or Cat #1104 instead of 'Soxy'. Humans, too, experience this depersonalization when referred to as 'the patient,' 'the policy holder,' 'the insured,' or 'the burn victim'.

The coffee maker and switch company lawyers argued that no matter how special the hearing dog was to Janice, it would be erroneous to apply the Rescue Doctrine to a dog, especially a dog that Janice Finley had no reason to believe was still alive when she ran into the burning home. Her actions to rescue 'a dog' were not what a 'reasonable man' would do. They said Janice had time to realize the danger she faced. Her actions were reckless and therefore, her injuries were caused by her own acts. She placed himself in peril and consequently her injuries were avoidable; they were her own fault. Further, had Janice exercised due care, Joyce would have no injuries.

The judge sided with the companies stating:

'The personal injuries and the emotional injuries and lost income of plaintiffs Joyce Finley and Janice Finley resulted entirely from their entry into the burning house. The actions of plaintiff Janice Finley in entering a burning home to rescue a dog are unreasonable conduct and she may not recover damages for any personal injury or emotional damages that she may have suffered. The actions of plaintiff Joyce Finley to retrieve her daughter were plainly occasioned by the unreasonable conduct of her daughter and not by any act of the coffee maker's. Thus, she is barred from collecting damages for her personal injuries, lost income, or emotional damages. Claims dismissed.'

After appeals that dragged on for ten years, Boomer's case was directed to a jury. The possibility of a jury trial convinced the coffee pot maker to settle out of court.

While Joyce and Janice's lawyer requested pain and suffering and emotional distress damages for the two women, they were not requested for Boomer. Their lawyer said that in those days, it would have been useless to ask. I agreed.

Privately, I remembered arguing in first year Property class that it was unreasonable to apply the 'reasonable man' theory to women who had a higher standard of 'reasonability'. The class thought the idea, as presented, was hilarious until Professor Diggs shot me one of his "I'll forget you ever said that" looks, without missing a beat in his lecture. If my exam grade was any indication, I think he forgot to forget.

The phone rang.

As soon as I picked it up, Arthur popped into auctioneer mode, speed talking. Did that mean he had good news?

"Carolyn, I found a great case. This is exactly what we need to support your sentient property argument. It's a custody case involving a cat between two…"

"Art, slow down. I can hardly understand you," I interrupted.

"Sorry. I'm excited about this one, though."

"Okay, but you're the one who's going to have to present this argument before the court. Practice being calm and collected now," I coached.

"Don't worry. I'll have my judicial face on when we get into the courtroom." Nevertheless, he took a long, deep inhale. "How's the weather in Vermont? Warm yet?"

"I can't even tell you how glad I am mud season is over. My wagon had to be pulled out of ruts hidden under two feet of mud. It looked like a turtle with its legs pulled in, sliding across the ooze on its shell. Moriah jumped out and became an instant mud monument—it would've come up past her head if I'd let her sink all the way down into the stuff." Most people don't know about Vermont's spring mud season. They find it hard to imagine how deep the goo gets on these dirt roads.

"But the lightening bugs are out," I continued on a more positive note. "Their show is worth the wait. There are thousands of them blinking in the blackness of our nights. No light pollution here. You should see them. It's magical." Hmm. It occurred to me that I was chattering on as if I still had cabin fever.

"I've mostly been chained to the computer though." With that I shut up.

"So have I. You'll never believe this case I found."

"Try me."

Arthur began. "For about a year, these guys, Greg Nivens and Jeff Beck, were roommates in Waxhaw, West Virginia. Their living arrangement stayed relatively peaceful until Jeff received a brown-striped cat, Max, as a gift from a friend who needed to find a home for him. Greg believed Max became partly *his* cat when they agreed to share his medical bills and other expenses."

Moriah gave me her inquisitive head-tilt look as our cat conversation continued. I covered the mouthpiece of the phone and 'meowed' at her just for fun. She launched into her high-pitched collie-bark. Then disappointed at my lack of follow through, she plopped back to the floor with a grunt.

Arthur barreled on. "Greg told the judge that he fed Max two or three times a day with little or no help. Max spent a lot of time with him. He slept in his bed. He functioned as his pet and he loved him dearly. But Jeff claimed the cat was his. He's on record admitting Greg took care of the cat, but the cat was given to *him* by his friend."

"Neither had ownership receipts for Max or his expenses," I assume.

"No. But when their lease ran out in May, Greg moved out and took Max with him. Jeff charged him with stealing his cat. The arrest warrant valued Max at less than two hundred dollars. A detective seized Max as evidence, and Max spent three months in the Animal Welfare League shelter," Arthur reported. "Greg visited Max sixty-four times and Jeff only twice."

"That speaks volumes about who cared for the cat." Moriah rose from the floor to stretch.

"The theft charge was dropped at the hearing because Max appeared to be jointly owned. Two weeks later, Jeff was able to persuade the judge to give the cat to him. The court said that while it was cognizant of the cherished status accorded to pets and the strong emotions engendered by disputes of this nature, it was best for all concerned that, given the cat's limited life expectancy, it should remain with the defendant, Jeff."

Arthur grunted, obviously frustrated with the decision.

"Life expectancy? What's that got to do with who should get Max or why?" It sounded ridiculous to me, too.

"There's more. Greg lost but didn't give up. He filed a civil lawsuit using witnesses who swore that he, not Jeff, was the cat's favorite. They testified that Greg was clearly devoted to the cat and had trained the cat to do tricks. Jeff argued back saying he had promised the friend who gave Max to him the right of first refusal, before Max could be given away to anyone else."

"Yea right. Sure he did. If that were true he should have said so in the beginning," I chimed in.

"I agree. Anyway, before rendering his decision, Judge Kenner took Max out of his cardboard carrier, held him in his lap and fed him a kitty treat. The judge said that if Jeff's friend had been present to testify that she gave the cat to him, Jeff would have had clear title. Given that Jeff's friend could not be present, Judge Kenner decided, "From what I have seen, Max would be better off with Mr. Nivens . . . Go with my blessing with Max the cat.'" Art meowed victoriously.

"That's a direct quote of the judge I take it? 'Go with my blessing with Max the cat.'" It *was* a novel choice of words.

"I think we can use this case. This judge considered the cat's feelings," Arthur insisted.

"Not exactly. He considered which human cared more for the cat. If Jeff's witness had shown up to verify ownership, the judge would have given the cat to Jeff regardless of what any of them felt, including Max. We can try it though. It may have value for us."

Arthur paused. I didn't mean to deflate his sails, but we had to look closely at these cases or we'd be sunk. "Let's keep searching, Art. There has to be something even better."

I needed to stretch and breathe. Moriah awoke with a startled look. Assuring herself that nothing was amiss, she extended her front legs in a leisurely stretch, attaining the canine version of yoga's downward dog position. I used to practice yoga positions and breathing. In through your nose, out through your nose. Some people breathe out through the mouth, but I read that breathing completely through the nose is more beneficial. This 'out through the nose' business will take some getting use to. I'll try it for a while.

Good news in, bad news out. Clean air in, dirty air out. Usefulness in, uselessness out. Victory in, failure out. It's easy to get lost in the breath. Breaking from work long enough to get started on deliberate breathing is the hard part. I get wound up, work until my nerves short circuit, and then push myself more. Christy and Shannon used to be my yoga teachers. They kept our class stretching and breathing. I wish they were here in Vermont.

Good thing I had Moriah. She was the only instructor I could afford while in law school. So many yoga poses were inspired by animals. I wonder why. She continued stretching and I followed her lead. We kept breathing, good luck in, bad luck out, until finally I felt energized enough to resume my position once more at the computer.

I scrolled down the list of unread cases. With a random (?) click of the mouse I found:

<u>Adam Bennett, for himself and as representative of his dog, Spirit, golden retriever, now deceased, Plaintiffs,</u>
<u>v.</u>
<u>East West Airlines, Inc., Defendant</u>.

Normally the case title would read:

<u>Adam Bennett, Plaintiff</u>
<u>v.</u>
<u>East West Airlines, Defendant</u>.

By including "Spirit, golden retriever, now deceased," this lawyer seemed to be making sure everyone would notice that this case was about an animal as much as it was about a human. More unusual, I had never, ever seen a case with a dog's name in the title as a plaintiff!

My hands tingled as I read and re-read "…for himself and as representative of his dog, Spirit, golden retriever, now deceased, Plaintiffs." Without reading another word, I knew this was the case we needed. This was THE ONE.

Who was the lawyer? I had to find out.

CHAPTER 6

The Visit

Finding information on Jolene Ruth Marion, Esq. was easy. As the founder of Legal Action for Animals, Jolene had acquired a reputation for tenaciously defending animals in court.

The information on the internet was pretty standard biographical fare.

She was born Jolene Ruth Steinberg on April 21, 1941, in the Crown Heights section of Brooklyn. She was the Granddaughter of Samuel Balinson, a Russian immigrant activist who founded the American Cloak Workers Union and wrote for the Yiddish Newspaper, *The Daily Foreword*.

Like her grandfather, Jolene was called ideological, intellectually gifted, highly principled and remote.

With an intelligence quotient of one hundred seventy-six, Jolene's academic, professional and social circles considered her a genius. She graduated *magna cum laude* even though her parents had died of unrelated illnesses while she was in school. Jolene and her father were estranged at the time and her critical mother never offered her much support. Marrying Michael Marion helped her focus on the positive and achieve academic success.

The couple hocked some of her mother's jewelry to pay for Jolene's law school entrance exams. As a law student, her animal interests emerged when she formed of the Lawyer's Committee on Animal Protection.

Following graduation from Seton Hall University School of Law, she litigated in Manhattan on behalf of urban animals in landlord-tenant disputes to allow the elderly and their companion animals to remain living together when they moved into federally funded housing. She fought for better treatment of laboratory animals and puppies raised in filthy puppy mills. She argued against leghold traps and animal sacrifice in religious rituals.

Though she lived on the modest income she earned as an Adjunct Professor of Environmental Law at Pace University, she regularly defended animals and their owners pro bono. This meant she took cases that were 'for the public good' but were uncompensated. Most of her clients had no money to pay her.

Jolene taught one of the first-ever Animal Welfare Law classes while at Pace. She also co-founded the Animal Legal Defense Fund, widely known today for its slogan, 'We May Be the Only Lawyers on Earth Whose Clients Are All Innocent'.

The New York State Humane Association presented her their Award for Humane Education.

For reasons unknown, I knew I had to meet this woman. I could tell Jolene was a progressive thinker, a lawyer from whom I could learn, if she would be willing to teach me. A lawyer who could help me help animals.

The next right thing seemed obvious. I just had to take action. As I packed the car for a trip to 'The City', Moriah cavorted in circles until I let her jump in. I was concerned about taking her because my car was a lemon. If I had a breakdown on a busy expressway.... I let her come but took all the precautions I knew—including extra oil and duct tape.

I swore I'd never own a car that needed duct taping. But by now, I was used to my 'I never's' becoming 'I must's'. At least I had the sense to buy blue duct tape, matching my blue wagon perfectly. New York City here we come.

By the time we maneuvered through clogged Manhattan streets finding the Francis-Lewis Boulevard exit, I'd reviewed the facts of her case as I knew them. Putting a dog's name in the title was just the first of a number of daring moves this lawyer made. And I was going to meet her!

Total, she'd brought five causes of action against the airline on behalf of Spirit and Spirit's young owner, Adam. Two were for Spirit's pain, suffering, and emotional distress. This was the kind of case Art and I were looking for. Two were for Adam's emotional distress over Spirit and the loss of her companionship. These causes of action were the heart and soul of her case.

A fifth cause of action originated with the airline ticket Adam purchased to fly Spirit back from Phoenix to New York. East West Airlines argued that the tiny print on the back of the ticket formed a contract. The small print contract confirmed an agreement between Adam and the airline that Spirit would fly in an East West Airlines plane as excess baggage with a maximum value of twelve hundred fifty dollars. Even smaller print told Adam he could pay additional monies to increase the value of his 'baggage'. East West claimed that Adam agreed to the contract simply by buying the ticket.

Contracts are unenforceable unless entered into by adults. The law assumes that minors under eighteen may not be able to fully understand the terms and duties of a contractual agreement. At seventeen, Adam was not

We've Got Feelings Too: Presenting the Sentient Property Solution

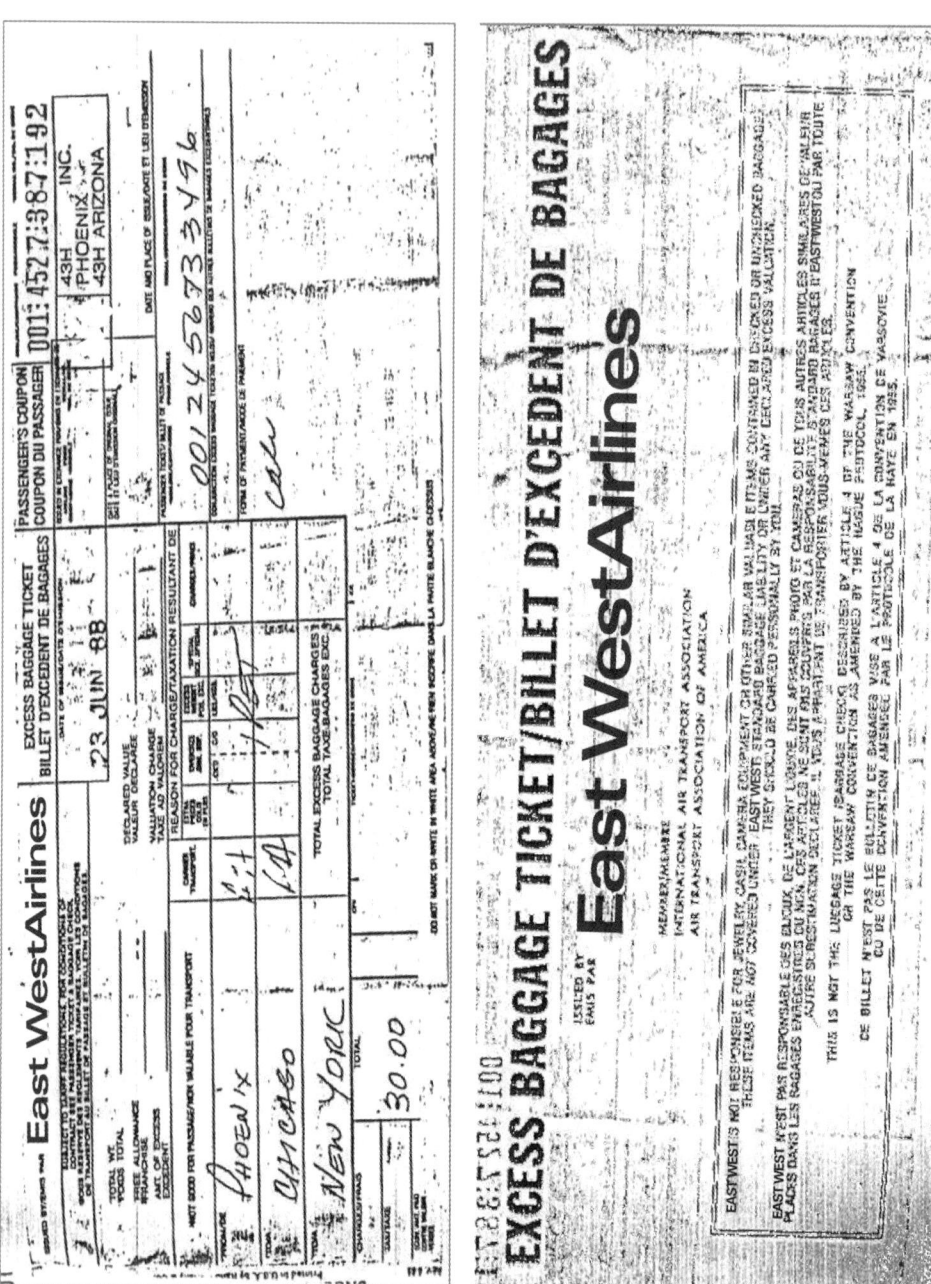

Front of Spirit's 'Excess Baggage' ticket.

Back of ticket containing small print 'contract'.

only a minor but a novice traveler. He could not be expected to understand the hazards of flying a dog in mid-summer in the hold of an airline 'at his own risk'. Therefore, he could not legally be held to the 'contract'.

Jolene had argued, further, it was the airline that broke the contract by failing to deliver Spirit in the same condition in which it received her. She requested damages of thirty thousand dollars.

That part was understandable. But even so, the case would be almost impossible to win.

Meanwhile, driving was becoming increasingly claustrophobic; sirens and horns mixed with hoards of determined people hurrying to important places. They flowed around my little wagon like a river, as if we didn't exist. These streets were made for horses and buggies, not a million cars. Adrenaline spikes frayed my nerves as we dodged one potential accident after another.

With Moriah still safe as my backseat companion, our expedition to meet Jolene began to take on the feel of an exciting odyssey. I played detective finding Laurelton, Queens then searching house numbers for the right combination, one-nineteen-sixty-eight. The morning was dark and overcast. Jolene was expecting me.

Down the block on the left side of the street, I noticed a car identical to my own in make, model, year and even color. Weird. It was Jolene's house; our twin cars were the first of many odd similarities between us. I parked, walked up the driveway and peeked inside. Manila folders stuffed with papers littered the seat and floor. Definitely the car of a busy lawyer.

As I rang the doorbell, gray clouds began to spit fits of rain. I thought I could barely make out the muffled sound of a woman moaning. I rang the bell again. Footsteps. Then voices. The rain picked up its pace, like a gentle horse moving from a walk to a trot. So did my heartbeat. "Mrs. Haversham" was all I could make out of the conversation inside.

I rang the bell a third time, and then looked at my watch wondering if I was early. "Mrs. Haversham?" Why did I know that name? The door opened.

"Are you Carolyn?"

"Yes."

"I'm Helena, Jolene's sister. I spoke with you on the phone."

"Yes, of course. Nice to meet you."

"Jolene is not well. However, she insisted on accepting your request to meet."

"I won't stay long. I just want to talk with her about one of her cases."

Helena smirked as if I had made a joke. "That's all Jolene ever talks about, her work."

She led me into a dimly lit living room with a large clock on the mantel above the fireplace. The seconds ticked loudly— tick, tick; quick, quick. The furniture suggested a time long gone. Each chair, table, couch and lamp radiated solidity, comfort and long service. The only piece of furniture less than a century old was a hospital bed with the head of the bed raised high—obviously one of those big, adjustable kinds.

A thin, pale woman lay curled up in the oversized bed. A bright red and gold velvet turban swaddled her head, suggesting royalty and vitality.

I could smell the truth. This woman was dying. I had smelled that thickness hanging in the air before. I never mistake death.

A third woman slouched in a green, frayed rocker beside the hospital bed, holding a book. She slid a medication tray in front of the weak form lying tangled in the sheets. Helena and I paused near the door as I took in the scene.

"Do you want me to finish reading to you, Jolene?" the woman in the rocker asked.

"No. I have *Great Expectations* memorized." The woman in the hospital bed rasped. She sounded mad like a hornet.

That was Jolene! She was the one who was dying. My heart sank. Helena had told me Jolene was not well. To me 'not well' meant the flu or some other incidental ailment. This woman was clearly dying.

Helena stepped into the room next to the huge bed. "Jolene, Ms. Matlack is here to see you."

I just stood there. In shock. The rain began to gallop. Even over the noise outside, the quick, quick of the mantel clock ticked incessantly throughout the room. Or could my heart be that loud? I moved further toward the deathbed so she could get a closer look at her visitor.

"Ms. Marion…"

"Call me Jo. My friends call me Jo." Each utterance was an accomplishment. She was obviously in a lot of pain.

The frayed-rocker-woman spoke up. "I'm Denise, Jo's nurse."

I knew that was my cue to say something but I couldn't. I felt an overwhelming sadness. Tears come so easily the older I get.

Helena interceded on my behalf.

"Ms. Matlack is working on a Michigan custody case involving a dog. She drove here from her house in Vermont to speak with you. She hopes your case with Spirit and Adam will help her case with Teddy."

Helena looked at me expectantly. The lump in my throat was still too big for speech.

"Are you ready to talk, Ms. Matlack?" Jolene rasped.

A direct question. I took a deep breath and stepped forward. "Call me Carolyn."

"Have a seat, Carolyn." Denise hopped out of the rocker and I assumed her post. She and Helena prepared to leave. "Jo, do you need anything else before we leave?"

It hit me just then. Mrs. Haversham was the reclusive old lady in *Great Expectations*.

"I still want to know what the doctors were whispering about yesterday," Jolene grunted.

"Let's talk about that later, Jo."

"Let's not. Damn it, let's talk about it right now." Suddenly, the docile invalid morphed into a snarling wildcat.

"Jo, you know I can't handle it when you get this way. Your mood swings…" Denise whined, seemingly in need of rescue.

Helena eyed Jo as she retreated cautiously toward the front door. She evidently knew her big sister well. At that moment the medicine tray went flying through the air, crashing against the wall precisely over the spot Helena stood seconds ago.

Jolene-the-wildcat raged against death with every cell of her being. "Just tell me what the doctor said!" she snarled.

"You don't want to have a fit in front of your visitor," Denise whimpered.

"Don't talk to me like I'm a child Denise. Just tell me what the damned doctor said," Jolene railed.

Denise broke down in tears. Solemnly, Helena answered for her. "Really, Jolene, you know what he said." The two sisters stared at one another. Nothing moved, only the clock with its never-ending, ruthless, merciless ticking. Jolene turned toward the dusty window on the far side of her bed. The rain hurtled against it blasting from the black, depressing sky.

Jolene's mood change flashed across the room faster than lightening. "Forget it." "My case!" "I must finish it—for Spirit, for all of them. Time to get into kickass gear."

Jaws clenched, only one tiny tear dripped over the side of her cheek and plopped hollowly on the sheet. She knew.

My eyes began to water. I was determined not to mess things up further by crying. "Maybe I should go. It seems I've come at a bad a time," I said.

Jolene moaned her lament.

As if on cue a yellow lab mix jumped dutifully into the bed and settled against her. The dog looked so solid and sturdy next to the frail occupant.

Jolene fastened her eyes directly on mine. "No, Carolyn, you've come just in time."

CHAPTER 7

Spirit's Story

"I need my notebook. I need to record the timing of these pains, see what the pattern is. FDR became President in a wheelchair, for crying out loud," Jolene struggled to sit erect. "There is so much left to do."

The other women left and we began talking. Her stamina humbled me.

Four hours later, Denise returned with groceries and office supplies. Helena arrived moments later. The two women had agreed to modify Jolene's room into an office.

"Drill a hole in the wall. I need electrical hook-ups for my fax and my computer." As the room makeover began, Jolene noted the birds strutting on the window ledge. She quipped, "Those pigeons are eavesdropping—ha, ha—get it? Eavesdropping?" With a feeble snort, she turned her attention back to me.

"What are you waiting for?"

Every detail of Jolene's case was of utmost importance to her. Although I had read the case carefully, I knew she could provide new and vital insights. Her urgency was contagious. Eagerly I sat like a sponge and listened. She began carefully reading to me from her copious notes, her story of Spirit and Adam.

"Spirit, a trusting golden retriever, lay dying of suffocation in her crate in the luggage compartment of a Jumbo 747 as it sat on the tarmac at Sky Harbor International Airport in Phoenix, Arizona. The date was July 23, 1988. Temperatures inside the belly of the airplane soared to one hundred forty degrees. Delayed for more than an hour, the plane had become a silver oven shimmering in the heat of the summer afternoon sun.

Seventeen-year-old Adam Bennett sat in the plane's passenger cabin unaware that his dog, Spirit, was in trouble. This was only the second time in Adam's life he'd been on an airplane.

Adam and his two best friends, Miguel and Jordan, were returning from a camping trip along the Apache Trail in the 30-million-year-old Superstition Mountains of central Arizona. Their Arizona adventure was a gift from their parents for graduating from high school with honors."

Jolene stopped and looked at me to make sure I was paying close attention. Satisfied, she continued her narrative.

"Adam gazed out of the window, watching the ground crews scurry about on the tarmac below. Men in their little trucks darted from hangar to plane and back again tossing passenger luggage onto conveyor belts. Bags and boxes lurched upward in soldier-like progression before pitching into the black interior of the aircraft. A baggage truck snaked into a quivering wave of heat, disappeared entirely and then reappeared like an apparition on the far side.

Navigating the airport had been as much of an ordeal to Adam as hiking the Superstitions.

Nevertheless, he had life knocked. He'd just graduated from high school, conquered a mountain then found this amazing dog. Life was good."

She looked at me again. "That's really one of the reasons I fell for this kid. He has guts. He had a tough time in school. Got bullied around. But he's a survivor. Class valedictorian. Then as soon as he gets to a time in his life where it seems he's enjoying himself, the stupid airline kills his dog," she hissed. The fire inside her was alive and hot.

It struck me that Fate had dealt just as unkindly with her as it had with Adam. "Were you happy before?" I asked.

"Before what?" she snapped back. I considered whether I should finish asking the question. She was so angry. I wasn't here to upset her.

"Before you found out you have cancer," I pressed.

"Things were going well. For the first time in a long time, life was good."

I wondered if she saw the similarity between her statement about her own life and the one she'd just shared about Adam. Jolene jammed a disk into her laptop. Three of her cats jumped off the bed and began to play cat-catch in the corner of the room. The toy flew away from their triangle. The gray one chased it under Jolene's bed. Jolene found the file she was looking for.

"This is one of the interviews I conducted with Adam." She handed me her laptop. Reading the file, I learned Adam was a soft-hearted, fairly naive kid up against a large airline that could care less what happened to him *or* his dog. "The law is supposed to protect the innocent and the underdogs. I *had* to defend him," Jolene broke in. I thought again about my sister and the long-ago rock episode. Another similarity between us.

"I'm tired of seeing people and animals treated like dirt. Someone should care that this dog died," she fumed. "The law should acknowledge that what happened to Spirit was wrong and punish the wrongdoer."

I wouldn't argue with that. Spirit died a horrible death. I read on as her account of Adam's interview continued.

"They met early on the fourth morning of the trip, barely sunrise and the light still faint. Adam lay awake on top of his sleeping bag relaxing in the quiet dawn. Just the day before, he and his buddies had prospected the great Silver King Mine deep in the Superstitions. His mind drifted to the possibilities for adventure in the day ahead. Maybe they'd hike up the canyon to see more petroglyphs."

Jolene stopped me again. "Talk about innocent. These kids were big into pretend games. One of them played Wyatt Earp; another Chief Seattle."

"Sounds like fun," I said more to myself than Jolene. She didn't answer, so I read more. I was enjoying the story.

"A few yards away, Miguel and Jordan slept soundly.

Then he saw it.

Peering right at him around a boulder, not fifteen feet from the end of his sleeping bag was a large dog. Adam described her as 'yellow, like the sunrise'. Two sets of soft brown eyes inspected each other. He whispered hopefully, 'Come here'.

The dog answered by padding softly over to him and flopping down on the edge of his sleeping bag. She was mostly golden retriever. Adam could see that beneath her matted hair, the dog was bone thin. She seemed exhausted and wore no collar. Yet her gentleness washed over Adam like the rising sun.

The dog was more than a welcome friend. The boys had survived a frightening event two nights ago. They'd been robbed by a sleazy-looking grizzled character who, thankfully, was only interested in their food. A real posse had galloped by searching for the thief who'd already stolen cash from near-by Apache Junction Savings and Loan.

Adam felt safe with her. Their need for each other created a strong and immediate bond. Adam gave her the name Spirit because she 'had a lot of life in her eyes'.

For the rest of the trip, Adam shared what food he had. She went everywhere with them. When they were rock climbing, she waited patiently at the bottom. At night, she never left their campsite.

Mornings he woke to find her lying close by, watching him intently for any sign of movement. They had a game. Adam pretended he was still sleeping. Barely lifting his eyelid, he peeked at her to see how closely she was really watching. She always caught him, her eyes shining with expectation; her whole body wriggled with joy just because he was alive and getting up for the day.

When only a week remained of their trip, the boys tried to find Spirit's original family. If that didn't work, Adam's mother had given him permission to keep her.

They put up notices in campsites and at the closest veterinary clinic. No one claimed Spirit. Two days before his flight home, Adam bought her a ticket and a regulation-sized crate. They gave Spirit a bath. All was ready for the trip home to New York.

Spirit didn't object to getting in the crate. Adam thought she knew, somehow, they were going home."

I stopped reading long enough to ask Jolene if I could take a break and let Moriah out of the car. She gave me a quizzical look, "Is Moriah *your* dog?"

"Yes, she goes everywhere with me. My car is her own personal kennel-on-wheels." Her look surprised me but I left to let my little girl out for a walk. Jolene began again before I shut the front door.

"The thing that still haunts Adam," she continued, "is the trust in Spirit's eyes as her crate was wheeled away. She trusted him to take care of her. He thinks he failed her by putting her in that crate on that airline."

I understood. Animals trust their owners with their lives. Spirit had been free roaming the mountains, yet was willing to go with Adam to a new place and a new life. Owning a pet is a huge responsibility.

Their story was only beginning.

"Sitting in the plane on the tarmac, Adam remembered that look. Unconditional love.

After an hour delay, the airline allowed its restless passengers to flock up the passenger runway into the cool waiting area where the boys continued to hang around.

When Adam realized he would miss his connecting flight out of Chicago, he asked an airline agent if he could see Spirit. Half an hour later the three boys still sat waiting. It was Miguel who cut through the line at the ticket counter and demanded action. "Why won't you get our dog? We've been waiting for an hour."

The agent summoned a blue-uniformed employee who motioned them to follow him. The boys trailed behind as he disappeared down the escalator to the baggage claim area and vanished through a rear exit. As Adam opened the same door, he was hit with a burst of air so hot and dry it made him blink. The hangar was broiling. Alarm jolted through him.

A baggage truck drove into the hangar. The blue uniform began sorting through a mountain of suitcases on the second of two trailing carts. Finding Spirit's crate, the uniform loaded it on a forklift and drove toward the boys. With a whir, the machine lowered the crate to the cement directly in front of Adam. Nothing could have prepared him for what he saw. Spirit had collapsed and was gasping for air. She lay convulsing and twitching in a semiconscious stupor. Her mouth was bloody, gums and paws lacerated from frantic attempts to claw and bite her way out of her cage-turned-prison. The airline had either forgotten she was there or ignored her entirely. Her kennel was a wreckage of blood, saliva, hair and skin. Adam held Spirit in his arms, a quivering heap of soggy fur, soaked in her own froth and blood.

No one at the airport would arrange transportation to a veterinary clinic. Two critical hours passed before Spirit received any medical attention at all. Another hour passed before they were finally driven to a hospital.

Day turned into a nightmarish hell Adam would never forget. Spirit lay suffering for hours on the floor of the veterinary clinic. Adam sobbed at her side, helpless to do anything but hold her head.

The veterinarian did everything he could. Spirit's brain was too damaged. There was no hope of recovery.

Dr. Jake Kingsley later described Spirit's symptoms in a written affidavit for the court. He concluded:

'In an area of a plane where the temperatures can rise to 140° Fahrenheit, a dog will become frantic as she tries to cool off by panting. Like panic attacks in humans. The muscular activity of the panting itself will increase the body temperature and add to the problem, which in turn further escalates the panting. As panic increases, she will become the canine equivalent of hysterical and will instinctively try to break free of her confinement. I have seen the description of the crate and how severely damaged it was. Due to observed trauma to the forepaws and a laceration on the tongue, it was obvious the dog attempted to chew out of the kennel. These are indications of the dog's panic and of how she was desperately trying to break free. During all of this time, she will experience extreme swelling of her cerebral fluids and brain tissues, causing brain damage as well as severe and continuing pain. A telephone call to any veterinarian would educe the advice to immediately immerse the dog in a bath of very cold water. Her initial temperature was 107° F. A delay of forty-five minutes before an ice bath is administered would reduce her chances of survival. During this long delay, she would continue to suffer enormously.'

Dr. Kingsley administered the euthanasia solution and Spirit quietly stopped breathing." I stopped to take it all in.

"What happened to Adam?" I asked, thinking what an awful guilt he probably still carried. I was done reading. I wanted to hear from Jolene directly.

"He was broken. Haunted by images of her trying to claw her way out of the cage. Imagine a dog so desperate to get out of a cage that she yanks teeth out attempting to pry open the bars."

"East West Airlines basically said, 'So what'. They took no responsibility for Spirit's condition."

Jolene made an obscene gesture at the airline.

I laughed at her. I didn't mean to, but I'm glad I did, because she laughed too. I guess she realized how awkward she looked wrapped up in the sheets, sick and weak, with both her trembling middle fingers poised upward against the world.

"Evil bastards," she hissed.

Laughing may have been inappropriate but the vision of this sweet dog trapped in her cage in the Arizona heat was just too much. For the airline to go on with business-as-usual and just write Spirit off as 'excess baggage' was enough to make one lose hope in humanity. We laughed to keep from crying.

Jolene's jaws clenched.

"Adam wrote letters asking for an apology. His letters went unanswered, so he began telephoning. The airline continued to ignore him. Adam realized he had to find another way to punish the airline. Carolyn, I tell you this kid was driven. If it took the rest of his life, he would stop this from happening to other animals." She winced and covered her mouth with her hand.

"Are you okay?"

"No, I'm not okay. Do I look okay? I can't even teach anymore—unless someone is interested in taking Titration 101." Another mood swing. She cut her eyes at me like I had stupid written on my forehead. I was used to it. My mother was better at it than she was.

Jolene grimaced. "I *am* Spirit. I know how that dog felt. I'm dying and no one gives a damn. I'm in a cage trying to claw my way out. When I'm gone, people will go on as if I was never here. Business as usual."

Hmm. Business as usual? I didn't know what to say.

Jolene was dying but she was obviously determined, or maybe fated, to work right up to her death. She seemed lonely, if not physically, then certainly mentally. Did she not have a husband or children? I had no husband or children. Perhaps by now, I should've known Jolene didn't either. Had she worked so single-mindedly at saving the animal world that she let her own life go down the tubes? I was afraid if I asked, she would feel even worse. I need not have worried. She brought me right back to the present.

"Why did you come here, Carolyn? You could have gotten this information at the court house. If anything was unclear you could have asked me over the phone. Why did you drive from Vermont to New York to ask me about this case? Don't tell me about this precedent you're trying to set with Teddy, the collie case. I want to know why you're *really* here."

She didn't blink. She wanted an answer now. "When I read the way you titled Spirit's case, I knew we thought alike." She stared, waiting for more. I had to dig deeper. "All my life, I have felt different from everyone around me because I knew what I wanted to do. I know a lot of people feel that way—different—so I wanted to meet someone with whom I shared common interests and goals; who cares about the same things I do. Perhaps I could learn from you."

I glanced at her to see how she'd take that. Her eyes were closed, so I wasn't even certain she was still listening. As much to myself as to her I explained, "I try to follow my gut without second guessing too much. I can't tell you much more."

The cats tired of their game of catch and bolted out of the room. The ticking clock grew loud again. Tick, tick. Tick, tick. How much time did we have left?

Jolene said nothing. The silence was uncomfortable.

When in doubt, focus on the work. That was all I knew to do at that point. "Where are you with the case now?"

Jolene looked relieved. Evidently work served as a refuge for her too.

"It's been six years since Spirit's death. There's no money in this case. I'm working pro bono. I can't work more than a few hours a day, even that's pushing it. I am trying to keep my job at Pace to pay the bills around here. I sent a letter to Judge Worley asking for a four-day adjournment."

"What did she say?"

"No."

"Did the airline move for dismissal?"

"Of course they tried."

"She denied the motion?"

"Yes, but she might as well have granted it. She gutted my case."

"When is she giving her decision?"

"Already did." Jolene handed me a copy of the judge's decision.

The Memorandum Opinion and Order came down from the United States District Court. Judge Worley dismissed the first four causes of action. In her view, they didn't legally exist! She'd seen nothing in previous case material that would allow her to consider the emotional distress of an animal.

Nor, she said, was there a separate cause of action for Adam's loss of the companionship of an animal. She relied on the old legal classification that Spirit was mere property, like a chair. Chairs don't have feelings, so legally neither did Spirit. And since animals are only plain personal property, Adam had no right to recover emotional damages for destruction of that property. It just had never been done.

The court went on to establish Spirit's worth by what it called her "market value." Since Adam had found the dog, he had paid no money for her. He had no official pedigree papers. Her market value was therefore zero. No one would pay anything for a middle-aged mutt.

The cost to East West for killing Spirit was four hundred dollars. The miniscule amount was certainly not enough to make the dog's death

Legal Action for Animals

239 Great Neck Road · Great Neck, NY 11021 suite 201
(516) ???-???? fax (516) ???-????

August 5, 1992

Hon. ████████
United States District Court
Southern District of New York
Foley Square
New York, New York 10007

Re: ████████ v. ████████
Docket No.: 92 Civ. 3740

Dear Judge ████:

We represent the plaintiff in the above cited action. Defendant has filed a motion for summary judgment which has been adjourned several times due for the most part to my having been on a medical leave.

Plaintiff's papers in opposition are now due to be served and filed on Monday, August 10th. This morning it became clear to me that I would not finish my papers in time, and I telephoned the attorneys for the defendant to request an adjournment of four days until Friday, August 14th. They would not agree to the adjournment.

Therefore I respectfully request that the Court grant me this short adjournment. I have been working on these papers to the virtual exclusion of everything else, but I had unfortunately slightly underestimated the time I would need to complete them when I proposed the current schedule.

Again, I sincerely apologize for any inconvenience this causes.

Thank you.

Respectfully,

Jolene R. Marion

cc: ████████
Attorneys for the Defendant

Jolene's letter to the judge

an economic deterrent to future 'deaths-by-airline.' It was far cheaper for East West to allow animals to die than to bother improving their animal-handling procedures. Neither East West, nor any other airline, had any incentive to change its policies regarding transporting pets.

"According to the court, Spirit was just a dog. We lost." Jolene hacked an awful cough as if the very admission to losing the case made her sick.

She gathered herself. "When the judge read the decision I knew my whole life was one long, bad joke. You're born, you work, you do good things, and then you die. What's it all for?"

"So is that it?"

"Is what 'it'?"

"With the case."

There was a long, slow sigh. "Technically, no. There is still the fifth and final cause of action. The judge did not dismiss the claim for breach of contract."

"That's great. That means the case could go to a jury. A jury might be more sympathetic. It wasn't over." I hoped that sounded encouraging.

Jolene neared tears, biting her lip. "I can't go to trial. Maybe we could win, but I can't see the case through. A trial would require massive amounts of work and time. I'm out of time." There it was. She admitted aloud that her life was nearing an end. The damned clocked ticked louder than ever. I wanted to take it outside, smash it on the sidewalk and kick the pieces into the gutter. Stop time!

"The radiation isn't reducing my brain tumor. If I can find someone else to take the case, hopefully they can see it through trial."

I hadn't known until that moment that she *had* a brain tumor. Nor did I know then that a brain tumor was only the last of a long list of cancers that had started with breast cancer, progressed to bone cancer, stroke and paralysis of her legs.

Tick, tick. Quick, quick.

CHAPTER 8

Research, Results and... Roaches?

The hotel was cheap by New York standards. Rank too. I had to be careful not to touch anything. Even the walls were grimy. I hated to think about what genus of wildlife stalked me in the carpet beneath the bed. I cleaned brown stains off the telephone mouthpiece before recounting my adventures thus far to Art.

"You wouldn't believe what I had to go through to get copies of the case." The United States District Court for the Southern District of New York in Manhattan was full of motions and correspondence on Spirit's case. I needed copies of it all to complete my research on Jolene's case.

"I couldn't take any papers outside the room to make copies. Six dinosaur-age copy machines lined the wall. They made copies one page at a time. Only one machine worked and each page cost a quarter! No wonder the pursuit of justice could so easily grind to a halt." Getting no response from Arthur, sympathetic or otherwise, I vented some more.

"I had to go beg for quarters from passers-by. The court house guards laughed. They thought it was funny. "Everyone hits them up for quarters," they joked. And wouldn't you know I hit the rain *and* the Manhattan evening rush hour trying to get back here? It poured the whole time!"

"Better you than me." Adam was finally being at least somewhat sensitive to my hard work. "How did the judge finally rule in the case?" I could tell Art was ready to move on.

"The judge dismissed the claims filed on behalf of Spirit. No pain and suffering for a dog."

"Did the judge indicate whether or not a claim brought by an animal was valid?" he queried.

"No."

"What about the claims filed on behalf of the kid?" He kept hoping.

"She threw those out, too," I reported. Art cursed and dropped the phone. I liked Arthur a lot, but too often he let his emotions get the best of him. Composure was not his strong point.

"The only claim left standing was the breach of contract." I wondered if he could hear me or if his malfunctioning cell phone was on the blink again.

"Because the airline didn't return the 'property' in the same condition as received." He was still with me.

"Exactly." A roach casually sauntered across the hotel dresser, like he was on his way to the movies. I turned toward the opposite wall. Roaches made my stomach flip flop.

"All of these cases so far are interesting but none allow a cause of action for an animal's feelings," Art said. "We'll have to create that precedent."

I thought, 'tell me something I don't already know'. Whoops. I was feeling abrasive, letting a case of New York nerves take over. Breathe. Patience in, rudeness out.

"The fact that these causes were even brought before a court do indicate the timeliness of our new proposed strategy," I reasoned. "I'm going to stay in New York another day or two."

Art protested. "Why? What else do you need to know about Spirit's case that warrants two extra days of research?"

"I want to talk more with Jolene."

"Who?"

"Spirit's lawyer, Jolene Marion. Have you heard of her?"

"Yeah. She's well known in animal law circles. Got a reputation for being something of a bulldog, hot-tempered." He definitely knew her.

"That's her, all right." I slipped out of my shoes and looked around for something clean to sit on. "I need to stay here with her for a bit longer."

"But why? I thought you were coming to Michigan this week. We need to prep for our argument ASAP." He couldn't understand what else there could be to talk about. I had the facts of the case and had discussed them with Jolene for hours, so I should move on. But there was more to learn and more to give. Sure we could talk on the phone. But for whatever reason, I *had* to stay a while longer. Jolene and I were both experiencing personal transitions as important as our legal interactions. We needed more time together—more face time.

"I'll be in Michigan by the end of the week. We'll have plenty of time to prep." That was that.

"Carolyn, I don't mean to be an ogre, but when I told you I would handle your travel expenses. . . ."

"Don't worry, Art. I'll take care of the extra hotel stay." In New York, that could quickly turn into a lot of money. I held my hand to my forehead to check my temperature.

"Okay. Well, be careful. I'll see you when you get to Kalamazoo."

I'm glad Art trusted me. He had a lot riding on Teddy's case. We all did.

My head began to throb. I knew this would be another sleep-deprived night. I turned out the light and began counting sheep. In hopes the old technique worked, I closed my eyes.

CHAPTER 9

Partners on the Path

"When we heard Judge Worley's decision, Adam could not understand how that idiot judge could throw out our claims—how she could even think Spirit was just excess baggage. I can still hear him loosing it."

Jolene detailed the scene weakly and without emotion. Perhaps she felt Adam had suffered enough for both of them or that if she let herself, she, too, would loose control. "This is not the first time I've been in the middle of an emotional maelstrom after a court decision. Adam's just one of many bereaved pet owners I've seen heartbroken by the law's lack of respect for animals and their owners. We both knew how strong the bonds are."

I watched her cats traipse through the house in bands and cliques. I'd lost count of them.

"How many cats *do* you have?" I finally asked.

"Thirteen cats, two dogs."

The cats ran the house. They were everywhere. Each cat in turn would leap onto her bed to offer purrs and nuzzles. She enjoyed a unique closeness with every one of her animals, making allowances for each of their singular personalities.

"I have to find homes for them, all of them. They're going to need somewhere else to live soon." Jolene certainly wasn't one for beating around the proverbial bush.

Neither was I when it came to animals and their lives. "What about Helena?"

Jolene stuck out her tongue as if she had a bad taste in her mouth.

"Won't your sister take care of your animals?" I asked.

"Maybe she'd take one. But then what about the other fourteen? Helena would never keep all of these animals in her house," she said. "One by one I'll find every one of them a great home."

"I'll take one," I volunteered.

"Not so fast. Don't think I'm desperate. I don't plan to give my animals to just anyone who asks. I have to know that he or she will take good care of them."

Jolene could bite where it hurt but I knew she didn't mean it personally.

"But I think I can trust you with one." By now, I'd learned if you didn't react, she softened.

Looking at Jolene I couldn't help but think again about the similarities between us; our cars, late schooling, divorce, no children, critical mothers and passive though loving fathers, younger sisters we felt compelled to protect, being physically strong, attending summer camp and now, above all, committed to helping animals through the law.

She could have been me. I could have been her.

So, near the end of her time on this earth, I wondered if she thought her life was worth it or was she really as bitter as she sounded. If she had it to do over, would she spend her life practicing in another area of law, open a small business, live in Nepal, or stay home with five children and bake chewy Halloween cookies?

I did *not* ask her if she was okay with the choices she made in life. I have tried to live my life so that when I get to the end—win, lose or draw—here are no regrets. I hoped like heck we shared this trait, too.

Jolene read my thoughts. She removed the red and gold turban from her head. She stared at me as she rubbed her patchy scalp.

"Chemo is a mother. I wouldn't wish this on my . . . I take that back. Yes, I would. There are some evil people in this world that *deserve* to rot from the inside out." I stared at her. She kept talking, venting. "They don't give a damn about anybody but themselves and they live large. What did I do to deserve this? Why do I have so much pain? Is God punishing me? Why? Why? Why? I don't get it."

She took her head in both hands. The injustice made her ache.

"Why does God hate me so much?"

"Has your life been that terrible?" I asked.

"Everything is such a fight. Every concession the world made for me, I had to kick and scratch to get." Her eyes kept asking why. She stared at me, waiting for me to answer.

"Some people have it easier than others. Rain falls on the just and the unjust." That was the best I could do.

She didn't accept it. Her mood darkened. "That's right. I keep forgetting. One cannot earn God's grace. It's a gift He bestows only on those who deserve it, not those who don't," she quipped sarcastically.

"Some questions don't have answers when we most want them. We just do the best we can with each day we're given, one day at a time." Her intellect prevented her from accepting such a simple response, but those were the truest words I could find.

She coughed up a wad of phlegm and spat in a cup stationed on the windowsill. "Whatever."

Helena appeared in the doorway. I hadn't heard her come in. "Jo, are you ready for lunch?"

"Not right now."

"Carolyn, would you like anything?"

"No thank you, Helena."

"Well, I'm leaving for class. Denise should be here before too long."

"I'll be fine." Jolene sounded exhausted. Her chemo made long work sessions impossible. Work seemed far from her mind at the moment.

"I'll call to check on you in a couple of hours." Her baby sister turned to leave.

"Seesta."

"Yes, Jo?" She hadn't been called the old familiarization of the word 'sister' since they were young. Lifetimes ago.

"Thank you. Thank you for everything—for who you are."

Helena froze. She couldn't remember such softness coming from her big sister whose role had been the always-right, always-strong older sibling. They locked eyes. Was it a soft, *loving* stare? Moments passed. Walls constructed over years crumbled in seconds. It was an honor for me to be present in the room.

Helena smiled, "I'll see you later."

Jolene plunked her red and gold turban back on her head with a flourish and straightened herself in the bed. "So tell me more about this case you have in Michigan."

I'd wondered if she'd ever ask. "What do the words 'sentient property' mean to you?"

"I don't have the energy for riddles." She cleared her throat of that awful goo and spat again. My stomach contracted, but I acted as if I didn't see.

I kept talking. "That's what we're going to argue in this custody case. While the collie is legally the property of one party, we believe he *wants* to live with someone else—someone with whom he has an emotional bond."

Jolene gave the notion due consideration. "Go on."

I found myself talking fast, as if we were pressed for time. Well, weren't we? "The case is about a troubled kid living in a group home that wants to use the collie, Teddy, for therapy. The kid's parents say, 'No way. The dog is ours.'"

Jolene closed her eyes. I rushed on. "The boy's parents say their dog is old and is in danger of being mistreated at the Home. Not only would they miss him terribly but Teddy would miss them—Teddy *wants* to live with them."

"So the court should give the dog what he wants?" she asked.

"In a word, yes. Teddy has feelings. They should at least be considered." My heart began leaping as the legal legs of my new theory were scrutinized by this veteran of animal wars.

If a major blunder existed, she'd pounce. Shortly she'd let me know whether she thought my work had possibility or whether she thought I was a delusional nut case. The worst case scenario was that I would have to go on without her considerable expertise, but go on I would.

"In a case about an animal who meets the definition of sentient property the court would be allowed to appoint a guardian *ad litem* if necessary, to represent the animal's best interests. This is nothing more than a court would do for any other individual deemed incapable of speaking for him or herself," I explained.

Jolene squinched up her face. "So what the hell is 'sentient property'? That's a new one on me."

"It's a new legal phrase. I borrowed the word 'sentient' from the European Union Treaty which states that animal are sentient beings. 'Sentient' means 'feeling'. In the United States, animals are categorized as plain personal property. Period. You know that was well as anyone."

"I know courts can only take baby steps to modernize law. So I asked myself, what could be the first realistic legal step toward creating greater respect for animals? What if there was a better classification of property—just for animals? Why not call animals sentient or feeling property?"

Jolene was in one of her moods. "No judge wants to hear your damned thought process! Give me a definition." She shook her head frustrated that I didn't answer her directly enough the first time. She cursed again for good measure, "Damn!"

"Sentient or feeling property is any warm-blooded, domesticated, non-human animal dependent on one or more human persons for food, shelter, veterinary care, or companionship normally kept in or near the household of its owner, guardian or keeper. Sentient property does not currently include animals kept for farming or activities regulated by the federal Animal Welfare Act."

Jolene didn't appear convinced. She kept thinking and I kept talking.

"I decided that there were two ways to make a difference for animals, through politics or the law. Not being a politician, I had to find a way, a practical way rather than a radical animal 'rights' way for courts to treat animals with greater fairness and respect."

"What's wrong with animal rights? What the hell is that supposed to mean?" I had offended her. She was volatile enough when she was in an even mood. Make her mad and there was fire.

I stepped lightly. "Jo, I have worked with animals in just about every capacity you can imagine. I had to accept the fact that animals' place in society is not equal to humans. Our society is comprised of meat eaters, poachers, hunters and researchers. Right now we *use* animals. That's not going to end overnight. Meanwhile I'm seeing animals suffer. We need a compromise."

"Don't you think animal rights activists work to end suffering?"

"Yes, but I know that animals will not acquire their own rights the way some radical activist groups have been demanding. I don't want animals and their owners to have to wait forever for justice. Society in general, not just animal rights activists, wants to treat animals better. We can make changes, but only a step at a time. All animals are sentient but we can start off with our companion animals. Sentient or feeling property categorization is a step we can take right now."

The room fell silent. I couldn't hear the clock anymore. Perhaps Helena removed it from the room after I left yesterday. One of the dogs barked at a blue jay as it lit on the window ledge. All of Jolene's animals seemed to be in the room keeping vigil.

"Your idea has merit," she finally conceded.

"You think so?" For some reason, I was surprised and pleased even though many other attorneys had told me the same thing.

"A new class of property, sure. I'm surprised I didn't think of it." Jolene began the struggle that was getting out of bed.

"You definitely fought for Spirit's feelings," I said. She slid out of bed and tried to get her swollen feet into slippers.

Jolene waxed morose again. Her disposition still shifting from moment to moment. "I tried. They threw my damned claims out, but I tried." She stood in front of an antique full-length mirror that looked like it had been shoved into its corner fifty years ago. Mrs. Haversham would have loved this furniture. I watched her hand shake as she lifted the sleeve of her bathrobe to dust the glass.

She was so weak. What if she fell?

"If there was provision in the law for sentient property, we wouldn't have to spend time convincing a judge that a dog should not be regarded as excess baggage—a suitcase for cripe's sake." She still blamed herself for loosing Spirit's case.

I wanted to tell her that it wasn't her fault. The fault was with the law.

"And snot-nosed lawyers wouldn't get to drone through patronizing arguments about animals not having the same rights as humans," Jolene said shuffling closer to the mirror. She still had fight.

If I kept her focus on sentient or feeling property, maybe she'd ignore the frail image staring back at her. "Right. We'll concede an animal can't be given the same rights as humans. But courts will recognize that animals have emotional lives and thus cannot be treated as if they were inanimate objects. There *is* an 'in between' compromise." I pressed on.

"Plus, when you can say that an animal is worth more than you paid for it, that's when we could get into big money. I *am* for setting limits on their monetary worth, just as we should for people. But you're right, when you call an animal sentient property, lawyers-and owners-could recoup higher levels of damage awards than they can now when an animal's worth is only its market value. We both know that market value is often nothing. Zip, zero, zilch, as my dad would say."

Jolene turned away from the mirror. "Why are you doing this?"

"What? What do you mean?"

She hobbled toward me. "What's this all about for you? Why are you pushing sentient property?"

"I don't understand," I stalled.

"Yes you do. What's in it for you?" She asked. I didn't answer. I thought we'd already been through this.

She sat down beside me to consider my eyes. Her nose wrinkled as if she smelled something bad. "When I was ten years old, my dad and I walked out of a movie where a man literally beat the shit out of his horse. Blood and horseshit covered the road." Her eyes withdrew as she remembered the scene. "To me it looked like the horse was trying to commit suicide using the rope he was tied up with."

Oh brother. Another similarity! We had both seen movies when we were ten years old showing an act of cruelty to an animal that left a life-long memory imprinted on our psyche. "That's the reason you take only animal cases?" I asked.

"Yes."

"That's the reason you work for free?"

"Yes."

"Never have any doubts or regrets at all?"

"No."

"All due respect, I believe you. But *I* have doubts and fears sometimes." It was important to be as honest as possible.

"Really?" She retreated toward her bed.

I watched as she gathered her nightgown at the hem, then back-rolled herself into bed. I could see that gathering up her sheets was too much of an effort. I slowly drew them together and tucked her in, half wondering if she would allow me to help or snap at me.

"Well tell me your reason, Carolyn Grace. How did you land in this animal rights battlefield?"

"I prefer to call it 'animal welfare battlefield'. I'm here for the sake of all animals, including my own, and owners like me who care about them."

"Did somebody put strychnine in their Puppy Chow?"

"Mine? No Peppy got hit by a car, but that's not why I'm with you today."

"Spit it out."

"Mostly because I love them. And, in some ways, I betrayed them. I didn't mean to, but I did." A storm of tears gathered behind my eyes. I hadn't learned to talk about this part yet. "I had a job doing cancer research at a university. I killed thousands of mice and other lab animals. Have you ever heard a rabbit scream?"

I rushed on. "My next job I was Production Manager at a beagle factory, raising beagles for laboratory research. So many products we use have been inhaled or worn or tested on or in an animal—from toothpaste to dog food. At the beagle factory, my responsibility was to raise ten thousand dogs a year to be shipped off around the world to people who experimented on them." There I'd said it.

Jolene moaned like the world was ending. I wondered if I should even go on. But I needed to finish. "One big toothpaste company hired us to brush the dogs' teeth three times a day. It was fun for them. They went wild with joy at all the extra touching and attention. But at the end, they all had to be sacrificed so company scientists could measure how the toothpaste affected their bone structure." I didn't even look at Jolene. Even her animals were still.

"I have nightmares."

"But you did it." Jolene's tone was softer than I expected, but her eyes sparked her disapproval.

"I did. After my divorce, I needed to support myself and work with animals…"

"And you didn't care what job you took."

"I cared very much. I believed I was doing good things. Who better to go the extra mile to care for those poor dogs than someone who loves them?"

Jolene had reservations, but by then I was not to be stopped.

"There was one little beagle bitch, a 'good breeder'. Her tattoo was BAO51. She'd lived for eleven years in a one-and-a-half by three-foot wire crate high up on the third tier of crates. The wire cages were suspended over plastic troughs that collected the tons of urine and feces as it fell through the wire cage bottoms to be flushed on a bi-weekly schedule out to a lagoon.

Because she had large litters of healthy puppies, she'd remained a breeding bitch her whole life. Every single time she went into heat, she had a litter. She did this crazed circle thing, running two steps across her cage, upside down around the top, down the side in a leap and back across the wire floor. Over and over. She went nuts every time I came near her cage.

I couldn't imagine what it would be like to live in that cage for eleven years and *never* get out nor be handled and petted. Ever. Her paws were deformed by living her entire life on wires. And the puppies…." I couldn't go on.

The light outside Jolene's window was fading. So much time passing. Quick, quick. Quick, quick. I surveyed the room. Everywhere I looked I saw BAO51. How could she give me those love-looks—me being her prison warden? I'd wanted to steal her and take her home. Let her live out her life with love. What happened to her? I couldn't handle knowing the answer.

My turn to go to the mirror in the corner and stand there, looking inside. A noise drew my attention downward. Ticking. The clock lay under the mirror. I knelt down and picked it up.

"I threw it across the room yesterday after you left," Jolene admitted. "But it didn't break."

I replaced it on the mantel.

"It is that little beagle's happiness and forgiveness that really haunts me. I can so identify with Adam."

Jolene's hound-mixed-with-something looked at me, rose and moved toward me. Her nose practically touched the floor; her tail wagging low and slow. As she flopped at my feet I patted her, giving silent 'thanks' for her show of support as I continued with my own narrative-turned-confession.

"These animals were going to get used for research whether I was there or not. No one could stop that train."

Jolene's hound lifted her head and licked my hand still sensing my angst. Moriah did that too.

"What's her name?" I asked.

"Mariah—like the wind." Jolene answered.

"Mariah!" It was one of those Moments. Could all our similarities be coincidence? What was going on?

"She's so sweet." I could hear my voice shake and fought for control. These emotions were wearing me out. "That's *my* dog's name, too. They call the wind Moriah. Only I spell Moriah with an 'o'." I was used to my own misspelling by now.

"I can tell she likes you," Jolene admitted. She wasn't finished with me yet though. "Why beagles?"

"Because they're medium sized, short-haired and friendly, easy to take care of."

Jolene gritted her teeth. "You worked for drug companies." It was more an indictment than a question.

"Yes. That was another job. Our division made drugs for animals. I did good work with them, but there were times I wanted to quit. I asked for guidance from a veterinarian who worked at the Humane Society of the United States in Washington, DC. I was beginning to think about quitting and going to law school even back then."

"I'll never forget what he told me. 'Carolyn, you can do more from the inside of one of the most powerful drug companies in the world than the next hundred demonstrators can accomplish from the outside. Stay and change policies and procedures from within, although no one will ever know you exist.' Since that part didn't matter, I stayed for another ten years."

Though Jolene was moody and judgmental, she nodded. From her I could handle it.

"Part of my job was to inspect the care of all of the animals that we used on farms and universities all over the world. I had to be very careful. If I had been labeled as a radical animal rights person, I would be fired or, at the least, no one would listen to me. I learned to work within the system. No glamour. Slow going. But in the long term, an effective way to achieve lasting change."

Jolene exhaled and for the first time truly relaxed. Every muscle in her body took a break. "The system… This world is so mucked up. Why am I fighting to stay in this life?"

"For the same reasons *I* stayed on the job, to help the ones who need you."

Jolene wilted further under the sheets, as if prepared to die post haste! I hurried to her side and pulled her up, a bit roughly, but it was an emergency. She was giving up.

I sat on the bed and looked right into her eyes. "It matters that you were here, Jolene. You changed a piece of the world when you wrote the title of that case, never mind everything else you've done."

She wept.

Her Mariah leapt onto the bed. I got up to leave the room. Jolene needed family around her. She needed to feel love, appreciation and worth in these last days. I was sure my nightmares, visions and plans brought no comfort to her at all.

She stopped me before I reached the door.

"Carolyn, don't leave."

"I don't want to upset you. You could use some rest."

"There's no time to rest. This has got to mean something. We have to make all this mean something." Jolene's will was rock hard, unshaken even by impending death. "We can win Teddy's case."

She'd said 'we'.

"Sentient property can work. All we have to do is prepare for every possible argument. Dispel every foreseeable fear. Naysayers will insist sentient property is a slippery slope to animal rights. I can hear them now, 'Is an earthworm sentient?' We have to know how to counteract this stuff." Her fingers crept toward her notebook. "Animals need this now. I've seen how they hurt."

I stepped back into the room.

I marveled at her strength. At the same time, the prospect of being partners in Teddy's case was thrilling. Dumping emotional baggage, while exhausting, was cathartic. "I'm ready if you are."

We talked, even yelled, argued, planned, wrote and strategized until sunbeams danced past the dusty window through the airless room.

A new day had begun.

CHAPTER 10

How It Works

Driving out of New York toward Michigan, I thought about Peppy, Spirit, Max, BAO51 and Moriah. Animals and animal-loving people deserve justice. I wanted to win our case in honor of them all.

If Teddy's case could create precedent, others could use the principle of sentient property. Penalties for harming animals would become much harsher.

Each person could help by just telling a friend that there is a new way to treat animals legally. The friend might tell a coworker who tells his neighbor who mentions sentient or feeling property to her daughter who hires the lawyer that . . . .

Small steps add up to big ones. As they say, first things first.

Crossing the Michigan state line, I did two things. I called my mother to say 'Hello' and that I was almost back in Kalamazoo, about to face the most exciting challenge of my life.

"I hope you do better with this one than you did the last one." She didn't seem interested. I wondered if she even wanted me to visit. Something in her voice sounded different—strained and distant.

"Are you alright, Mom?"

"Oh sure." That was her standard answer. She could be feeling terrible but she wouldn't talk about it. Alarm bells rang. The conversation ended.

Ouch. More hurt.

The voices in my head started their familiar rebuke. "You idiot. You just did it again. When are you going to grow up and learn? You're not going to get encouragement from your mother." I call this uninvited gathering 'the Committee.' They can get loud and unruly. I told them all to 'Shut up'.

The second thing I did never fails—pray.

CHAPTER 11

Teddy's Case—Part Two

"There is only one issue before us: whether to allow an animal—Teddy, a collie dog—to be represented in court under substituted judgment doctrine as sentient or feeling property, thus allowing consideration of the dog's own feelings in legal decisions affecting his destiny." Judge Matthew K. Lewis set the rules right up front.

Our job was to convince Judge Lewis of the necessity of considering an animal's feelings, show him how it could legally be

*Important Note: Teddy's Case as depicted in Chapters 4, 11, 12, and 13 is based on extensive legal research by the author about what *could* happen in a real court situation using sentient property to show animals greater compassion and respect. These four chapters are the 'blueprint' alluded to in the Introduction. Teddy's Case is but one example of sentient property's potential use. It is meant to be a compelling model and has not happened—yet.

done and then ask him to appoint Arthur to do it. Suddenly, the task looked gargantuan.

Judge Lewis exhibited an affable yet stern demeanor. "Is everyone present, Mr. Jackson?"

Arthur was calm and cool. I was impressed. "Yes, Your Honor. Teddy and his team are all here."

Total there were eleven people and one dog in the crowded judge's chambers. Unaware he was the main attraction, Teddy snoozed peacefully on the floor in front of Judge Lewis's well-worn mahogany desk. The man who would decide his future continued.

"The issues prompting this proceeding are uncommon but not unheard of in a court of law. More and more frequently the courts are being asked to resolve animal-related issues, and I recognize a growing disappointment by society in our adjudication of these matters."

All present focused intently on the judge as he made his introductory remarks.

"This court in no way aspires to examine, much less resolve, issues surrounding animal rights. However, changes in the convictions held by our society and recent legislative activity in many states regarding protections for animals suggest that this court should consider whether to give comparable scrutiny to the destiny of one animal, Teddy, the Sullivans' collie dog as it did to their son, Ralph Sullivan."

"As you are all aware Ralph Sullivan's custody case resulted in this court's decision to order Ralph Sullivan be permanently relocated to Pine Haven Home for Boys. The Home is now requesting permanent custody of Teddy for therapeutic use. So Mr. Jackson, please begin."

"Your Honor, Carolyn B. Matlack, J.D. will be the first speak to the court on behalf of Teddy's team," Arthur said.

No objections, so I got up.

"Thank you, Mr. Jackson. Your Honor, I will demonstrate to this court that it not only is desirable but entirely legally feasible to appoint a guardian *ad litem* for Teddy and to allow an attorney, Mr. Arthur Jackson, to represent Teddy's best interests using substituted judgment doctrine. Teddy is not just a thing, but a living breathing sentient being. Further, we will introduce the legal phrase sentient or feeling property. Placing a dog like Teddy in this higher category of property will allow the court to consider how the animal himself feels about his future residency in this custody decision."

"Following my comments, Jean M. Louder, Professor Emeritus of Law and Philosophy, International Law School, will discuss the ethical implications of using the Doctrine for Teddy. Together, we will show that it is both appropriate and reasonable to use the Doctrine for a dog. I will begin with a short look at history."

I went into the zone. There was no one there but me and the judge. "Substituted judgment has been recognized and used as a form of legal fiction in American courts since at least 1844. Courts use legal fiction when they allow a guardian *ad litem* to speak for those who cannot speak for themselves. For example, a six-month-old baby cannot speak for himself or herself. Instead, the baby 'speaks' through her parent or legal guardian. This is legal fiction in action. It is her guardian *ad litem* or qualified adult who substitutes his or her judgment for that of the baby."

So far, this seemed far easier than moot court in law school. There, five black-robed judges perched in a row like ravens peering down over the front of the bench as each legalwannabe took their turn presenting a case, orphaned behind a lone podium. My notes lay untouched. Breathe. Calmness in, nervousness out. I slowed down.

"The list of those not allowed to speak for themselves in court is long; those convicted of a felony, members of a 'shameful trade', members of a lower caste, members of a different race such as African or Native Americans, deaf mutes, unborn babies, minor children and women. By not allowing these groups to speak, the court in effect imposed incapacity on them. Nothing new to you, Your Honor. Ralph Sullivan's case is familiar to us all," gesturing around the room.

I paused. I could actually see myself delivering my remarks—like an out-of-body experience. That's how easy it was.

"The Doctrine has also been used for nonhumans. In 1868 the Supreme Court of the United States held that *a ship* was guilty following a collision. In effect, the court assigned personhood to the ship, based on the ship's potential for causing harm. The court said this was not a case against the owner but against the ship. The collision was committed by the ship without the authority and against the will of the owner."

"We are asking the court to appoint Mr. Jackson to speak for Teddy using the Doctrine of Substituted Judgment."

Teddy raised his head when I mentioned his name. I took a second to look at the dog; a beautiful collie, obviously well cared for. Moriah and Teddy would probably love to pal around together.

"So we see that our legal system has both granted and denied certain individuals the right to speak in court. I do not need to remind you, Your Honor, but for the rest of those present, courts of law create legal protections when protections are necessary. The reason is simple. It is the duty of the courts and our laws to protect those unable to protect themselves—the greatest fundamental principle in our judicial system."

"Examples of courts reshaping common law to new thinking in changing times are numerous, especially when there is a strong sense that justice and the public welfare demand it."

Judge Lewis was staring right at me. No reaction. We were taught in law school that if judges were buying your argument, they would interrupt and ask questions. Maybe I was doomed after all. I plunged on.

"History reveals that the process of reshaping law is an evolutionary one. It begins with public discontent. Discontent leads to civil unrest, with episodes of civil disobedience. Meanwhile, courts find it increasingly hard to apply outdated law to modern cases."

"Common law thinking evolves and becomes the new standard. New legislation is passed. Then we again look to the courts for interpretation of the new legislation. The process is circular and endless, as it should be." I paused. Quiet. I'd totally lost him. No choice but to go on.

"A good example is Mothers Against Drunk Drivers or M.A.D.D. Outraged that horse-and-buggy laws did not effectively address drunk driving accidents, they brought case after case forcing courts to recognize and respond to deficient, outdated law. Look what's happened since."

The judge smiled but not at me. He leaned over his desk looking at Teddy. For a millisecond, I felt warm sunshine break through. The whole day and now the whole argument was making sense. I relaxed. It would work out like it was supposed to.

I told him about Spirit, Boomer, Nala and Max. I presented facts about Leo, a bichon friese who was thrown from his owner's lap by a driver in a fit of road-rage who threw the little white dog onto the highway where he was run over and killed. Each case demonstrated animals and people whose feelings and emotions were obvious and where courts used, or were at least exposed to, legal principles in a creative manner to reach fair and just decisions.

These cases provided background for our argument that Teddy had identifiable feelings and they mattered—ethically, morally and legally.

I glanced at Arthur. His wink was imperceptible to anyone else in the room. He knew that the core of our logic was coming up next. We had rehearsed this a hundred times.

"Today in this room, as we consider the use of the Doctrine of Substituted Judgment for Teddy, we are progressing toward a civil solution that befits those sentient beings we can rightly call sentient or feeling property."

Judge Lewis finally broke his silence. "Can you give us any guidelines to determine what animals may be classified as sentient or feeling property?"

"Yes, Your Honor. A finding that an animal is sentient property shall be determined only after assessing the depth of the relationship between owners and their animals. In determining the existence of such a bond and the monetary value of such property, Your Honor could consider the following criteria:

1) The duration and continuity of the relationship between owner and animal,
2) Unique behavioral characteristics and special needs of the animal,
3) Special needs of the owner,
4) Multiple events or occurrences demonstrating the bond of friendship, trust, and loyalty,
5) Evidence that the animal in question has:
   a) Been examined at appropriate intervals by a veterinarian, provided with preventative medical care, and treated for any illnesses, injuries or conditions requiring medical care,
   b) Been fed, groomed, housed, and maintained in a safe envronment and in good physical condition unless it has or has had an injury or illness not brought about by the owners' negligence, and the owner has followed medical advice to provide any requisite treatment,
   c) Had no less than weekly contact and interaction on average with the animal's owner,
6) The classification of an animal as a service or therapy animal shall be presumed to establish the existence of a strong human-animal bond, unless evidence can be introduced to the contrary,
7) Medical evidence that the owner suffered emotional distress or mental anguish as a result of an act(s) of cruelty or inhumane treatment of an animal.

Once the court declares an animal to be sentient or feeling property, we suggest a three-part test to decide when to use the Doctrine of Substituted Judgment in an animal case. We call it *Teddy's Test*, for obvious reasons." As if on cue, Teddy rose from his spot in front of Judge Lewis and surveyed the room. Finding nothing of interest, the old dog slumped back to the floor with a weary sigh.

"The Doctrine may be used when:

1) The owner of sentient property needs to redress a harm that caused or may cause pain and suffering or emotional distress for the animal or,
2) The owner of sentient property needs to redress harm for personal pain and suffering or emotional distress due to the loss of or harm to their animal or,
3) The interests of the sentient or feeling property need be weighed between that of the owner and that of the greater good of society."

I was almost through!

"Your Honor, I am not requesting that you grant Teddy unlimited legal rights. Nor am I proposing a radical shift in the way animal cases are handled by the courts. To the contrary, I seek the court's consideration of a middle-ground approach."

"Should you permit Teddy to be classified as sentient property, Part One of the test allows the court to consider Teddy's feelings in the matter of his living arrangements. And Teddy would remain the property of the prevailing party in this action. Under Part One, emotional distress is a permissible cause of action for an *animal* so categorized or, under Part Two, for the *owner* of an animal categorized as sentient property. Some cases may require a court-appointed guardian *ad litem* to speak on behalf of the animal. It is important to recognize that not all animals fall under the category of sentient property. Cases are limited largely to owned companion animals, that is, companion animals who are private sentient property."

The other lawyers scribbled notes. Arthur slipped me the thumbs up signal. I was down to the last sentence.

"Sentient or feeling property is the next reasonable legal step toward greater fairness and justice for animal owners and the animals themselves and recognizes the important, critical roles they play in today's society." I took my seat. The ceiling fan whirred. Pine Haven's attorneys whispered among themselves. Arthur stepped forward.

"Mr. Jackson, do you wish to continue?" Judge Lewis queried.

"Yes, Your Honor." I'll start off by saying that some legal scholars argue that animals deserve 'personhood'. Good idea or not, I do not think our courts are ready to go that far just yet."

Judge Lewis guffawed at the notion. "Personhood?"

"Again, what we are proposing is a middle-ground approach. *Teddy's Test* can be used to decide which cases can use sentient property and the Doctrine of Substituted Judgment for an animal. We have seen common law change throughout history so that it remains current and practical…" The judge motioned for Arthur to stop.

"Mr. Jackson, can you come up with some relevant case law? You know as well as I do I need to see some precedent here. You're expecting me to stick my neck out by being the first to grant sentient or feeling property status to an animal and then use the Doctrine. Tell me, just how swiftly is my head going to roll?"

"There is current case law for you to consider, Your Honor. And more of it than ever before. Animal-related law is experiencing change. In a 1993 decision, following a lengthy legal battle in the Pacific Northwest over the salmon being unable to swim upriver past the dams, the Ninth Circuit said that fish were wards of the court under Article III of the Endangered Species Act. As with any other ward, it is part of the court's responsibility to ensure that the listed species will be adequately represented by counsel who will advocate its rights and seek its protections to the fullest extent of the law."

"This case is distinguishable from Teddy's case because it pertains to rights for listed animals under the Endangered Species Act. However, when the court found salmon to be wards of the court deserving of representation and protection, the court's decision reflected not only the letter of the law but society's growing recognition of the importance of an individual species, if not an individual fish."

"Wasn't there a fairly well known Texas case?" Judge Lewis was asking questions again. A good sign. I tried not to get excited.

"Yes, Your Honor," Arthur forged on. "In a 1983 Texas divorce action, the trial court made the wife managing conservator of their dog, even though managing conservators were created for human children, not canines. Reasonable visitation rights were also awarded."

"Mr. Jackson, how much more time do you need to finish?" And by the way, taking up the court's time for animal cases puts an unmanageable burden on our already overcrowded legal system. What do you say to that, Mr. Jackson?"

"I am ready to conclude now, Your Honor. The answer to your overcrowding comment question is, 'I agree', Your Honor, the courts are admittedly overburdened. But correction of this condition should not come at the expense of justice. We suggest using *Teddy's Test* to decide which cases should be heard."

"In conclusion, our legal system exists to provide fair and just solutions to problems in today's society. Our animals are a huge part of our society. We are not asking this court to change Teddy's basic legal status. He is already considered property and we do not dispute that. But we do request that the court raise his status a notch to sentient or feeling property allowing the court to use *Teddy's Test*. By designating me Teddy's guardian *ad litem*, our team will apply the aforementioned Doctrine to bring about a legal decision that neither grants Teddy unlimited legal rights nor repudiates them outright."

"Having been granted the opportunity to be heard, Teddy and I will propose that he is happier with the Sullivans and therefore should remain the sentient property of Mark and Laura Sullivan."

Judge Lewis stood up. Everyone else followed his lead.

"Thank you, Mr. Jackson. Following a lunch break, we will continue with statements from your expert, Professor Louder."

I headed straight for a phone. So far, we were still hanging in there. I couldn't wait to talk to Jolene.

Helena wouldn't let me speak to her.

"Why not?" I wanted to know. My gut gave the answer before Helena could even respond.

"Carolyn, she can barely breathe. She can't talk, right now."

"But we have a chance to win. She *has* to know that. Tell her we could win this case!"

"I will," Helena promised.

That wasn't good enough. "Right now. Tell her right now."

I didn't care that I was being pushy. I wanted Jolene to smile before she...moved on. I could hear Helena relaying my message.

Helena turned her attention back to the receiver. "She's very pleased about that, Carolyn. She wants the phone. Hold on."

"Carolyn?" I could barely hear her. In just days her voice had deteriorated to a murmur. "I can go now."

"What?"

"I found an attorney . . . to litigate . . . final claim . . . for Spirit . . . Adam." Each word was an accomplishment. Jolene Marion was at the end of her earthly journey. "I . . . can . . . go now," she dropped off.

I didn't want Jolene to leave. Not yet. She was at once my mother, my sister, my best friend, my success and my failure. Knowing her had given me the gift of greater self-knowledge. Knowing her had been cathartic. She'd helped us prepare Teddy's case.

She was trying to speak again.

"You keep . . . Carolyn. What you're doing . . . good."

I couldn't catch it all. "We still need you, Jolene. There's much left to do. You're so good at it." You're supposed to tell dying people that it is okay for them to go, yet I so wanted her to be here for the outcome of our case.

She sounded resigned. "I'm not . . . special. I'm . . . ordinary woman, with strengths . . . fears, like you. Guess I've . . . done my part."

"Thank you, Jolene. You made this possible. Thanks for everything."

This might be the last time we spoke, but the next phase of the hearing was about to begin. I had to be there.

Professor Jean Louder, a petite, authoritative woman, spoke first.

"Good afternoon and thank you, Your Honor. Perhaps here, right at the beginning of my comments, is the best time to clarify what I am *not* saying as I present the ethical case for the use of the Doctrine of Substituted Judgment on behalf of animals. I am not asking that we refrain from eating meat, or that we stop using animals in medical research. I do not claim that animals are or are not biologically comparable to humans. I do not espouse rights for animals equal to human rights. Though I feel strongly about these issues, the discussion of them is not appropriate here today."

"What I do advocate is using the Doctrine of Substituted Judgment as a next step toward fair legal solutions for animals."

Mr. James Edison, Pine Haven's attorney, voiced his skepticism in three words. "On what grounds?"

The professor didn't blink. "Justice and kindness has prompted some advocates for animals to propose a Constitutional Amendment to recognize civil rights for animals. Perhaps, instead, a Constitutional Amendment to reclassify animals as sentient or feeling property would be in order."

Mr. Edison smirked. The professor ignored him.

"It is true that our Constitution does not refer to animals. It refers to men," she conceded. "But the fact is that we have already radically altered the meaning of 'men' from the time when our Founding 'Fathers' used the term. To them, the term meant 'adult white males'."

Judge Lewis encouraged the professor. "That's true."

Mr. Edison leaned forward in his seat and lifted his pen to object but the judge waved him off.

"The Founding Fathers spoke of the inalienable rights of all men yet society was without the most basic rights for African Americans, Native Americans, children and women."

"Even the wives of the Founding Fathers were denied most of the rights their husbands enjoyed. They could not own land or inherit property; in fact, they themselves *were* property! In 1776 Abigail Adams, wife of the future President John Adams, wrote him an impassioned plea. Allow me to paraphrase what she said."

> 'In the new Code of Laws which I suppose it will be necessary for you to make I desire you would Remember the Ladies, and be more generous and favorable to them than your ancestors. Do not put such unlimited power into the hands of the Husbands. Remember all Men would be tyrants if they could. If particular attention is not paid to the Ladies we are determined to foment a Rebellion, and will not hold ourselves bound by any laws in which we have no voice or Representation.'

"If animals could talk Your Honor, they might say the same thing!" Professor Louder was brave.

"Calling his wife saucy, she continued, "Adams answered that he knew better than to repeal Masculine systems. To which Abigail retorted that while her husband proclaimed peace and good will to Men, emancipating all nations, yet he insisted upon retaining absolute power over wives."

"Abigail's wishes came true—although not for another hundred years after she died. In 1920, women received the right to vote with the passage of the Nineteenth Amendment to our U.S. Constitution. As you know, Your Honor, this was fifty years after African Americans were emancipated at the end of the Civil War."

Mr. Edison could sit still no longer. "Your Honor, this is totally off-subject. What does all this have to do with the dog?"

Ignoring him, Professor Louder addressed the judge. "The point is that the definition of 'men' as it is used in our Constitution, has evolved to include others, not just men."

I could tell Lawyer Edison had never owned a pet. In his mind, Ralph Sullivan's name on Teddy's registration papers proved he owned the dog—end of discussion. He probably thought this hearing should have lasted all of three minutes.

"Whether or not a Constitutional Amendment for animals is ever passed, there *will* be some legal response to the vast majority of United States' citizens who believe animals have feelings and deserve better treatment. It's already beginning to happen. We are merely offering a uniform legal method to allow it to happen." The professor scanned the room daring anyone to challenge her statement.

Mr. Edison continued his opposition. "But how can you advocate improved legal treatment of animals yet condone their use and destruction? What if an animal rights activist tried to use the Doctrine to represent a beef cow about to be slaughtered for food? Could the cow sue the feedlot owner?" Now it was his turn to scan the room searching faces for support.

Judge Lewis broke the silence. "I don't think that's what the professor is suggesting."

"Thank you, Your Honor. By proposing the use of sentient property, I am neither condoning the use of cows or other animals nor advocating their destruction. That is another debate for another case and time. Nor can I address all the future challenges to sentient or feeling property other lawyers will raise in court. As Ms. Matlack has clarified, argument and challenge is the substance of our legal system. This is the ongoing job of lawyers, no matter what kind of case they are presenting."

"Having said that, in my opinion if someone wanted to bring an action on behalf of a privately owned, pet beef cow and I was the judge, I might argue the third, greater-good-of-society, prong of *Teddy's Test*. I might balance the harm of slaughtering the cow against the harm of not slaughtering the cow to a society that needs or wants meat."

"Your Honor, applying the Doctrine to this case sets a dangerous precedent. What would prevent an activist from purchasing hundreds of cows just to save them?" Mr. Edison argued.

"What prevents them from doing so now?" Judge Lewis asked.

Wow. Was there hope?

Mr. Edison didn't have an answer, so he shifted gears. "But aren't Teddy's feelings—or sentience, as you call it—isn't that nothing more than reflex or instinct? Are you saying that he has feelings on a par with human feelings and that he thinks and reasons?"

I could answer that one. "May I speak to that, Your Honor?"

"Go Ahead."

"I have many examples of studies that prove animals think and reason. I will be glad to obtain copies for you and Mr. Edison if you'd like."

Teddy had moved and was lying next to Arthur. His would-be guardian scratched his ears. Teddy responded with pleasure groans. Still petting the old dog, Arthur asked "Just to follow up on that idea Professor Louder, in your professional opinion does sentience require intelligence? Do you have to be smart to feel?"

"No, you do not. Intelligence is the ability to learn. Feelings, at their simplest, are responsive recognitions to a stimulus. Sentience implies only feelings."

My mind drifted to Laurelton, Queens. I pictured Jolene close to death struggling harder to breathe, as we sat here in court arguing the fate of a canine life.

"Aren't you then limiting the use of the Doctrine to those sentient beings whose feelings we can evaluate?" the judge asked. "If so, how are these feelings to be measured or ascertained?"

"Recall the factors in Ms. Matlack's definition of sentient property," Professor Louder advised. "And, *if* additional evaluation is necessary, expert opinion is available in the form of behavior experts just as it was for Ralph Sullivan.

Mr. Edison interrupted again. He was losing his cool.

"Animals are not similar to humans," he shouted. "This is ridiculous!"

The professor maintained her composure. "Animals *are* similar to humans. That is the very reason they are used in research. Were they not similar to us they would not be used."

"Everything you say may be true…"

"Excuse me, Mr. Edison, I wasn't finished." She turned politely to address Judge Lewis once more. "Your Honor, Attorney Edison's instinct argument exemplifies how animal suffering is rationalized if we think of animals as unintelligent, unaware creatures."

Mr. Edison moved forward, his impatience mounting. "Your Honor that sounded like a personal attack. I'm not a callous, unenlightened man bent on torturing animals. But even if we wanted to there is no clear way to determine what Teddy feels. There's just no way to tell if he wants to live with Ralph, or the Sullivans, or run off with the circus!"

"We disagree!" Arthur, the professor and I all protested in unison.

"Your Honor, professor, if I may." Arthur seemed to be enjoying himself. "The question put simply is, *can* we tell what Teddy wants? The answer is, 'Yes'. We use the same techniques that were used by the court to determine Ralph Sullivan's preferences."

In Ralph's case, I knew the court viewed a video diary taken over a two month period showing Ralph living in the Sullivan home and in Pine Haven Home. The video was used as evidence in the court's decision to relocate Ralph to Pine Haven Home.

Our video diary of Teddy in the same two homes, confirmed that anyone, expert or not, could see the difference in his behavior living at the Sullivan's compared to Pine Haven Home. Eating or playing, Ted was happier with Laura and Mark.

Even Judge Lewis expressed surprise. "I have to admit, when I saw the tape it is almost easier to identify this *dog's* likes and dislikes than it was to figure out Ralph Sullivan's."

Dare we begin to think Judge Lewis might rule in our favor?

Professor Louder underscored our conclusions. "Teddy's tapes, evaluated by trained, certified animal behavior experts, show clear preferences. If we take the time for patient observation, we can identify Teddy's feelings. Behavior reveals feelings. Where does he eat best? How happy is he to see the boys on his visits to Pine Haven? All we have to do is observe."

Judge Lewis again interrupted. "Some would say animals have no morality or conscience and do not deserve enhanced legal status."

Professor Louder stood up again to address the court. "I'm glad you mentioned that, Your Honor. Some people do say that. They say that man (or woman) is the only one who knows right and wrong, yet many animals exhibit unmistakable evidence of moral behavior."

"That animals have a conscience or moral sense of right and wrong is supported by many recorded acts of altruism. Dogs have rescued people from fires and children from holes in the ice; wolves in a pack in

Alaska brought food to their injured leader each day until he was well enough to hunt with them again."

"Pet owners will swear to you that dogs display guilt when they have done something wrong. Personally, when I arrive home I can easily tell whether my dog, Andy, has upset the trash or chewed my pillows. He hides in the place farthest from his misdeed and remains the picture of contrition in a way that my other property—my suitcase or my television set—does not."

"If you have no further questions Your Honor, I request that Mr. Jackson be allowed to proceed as Teddy's guardian *ad litem*, to determine where Ted wants to live. Thank you." The professor took her seat.

"It's late. Let's recess until Monday." Judge Lewis wasn't the only one who was tired.

Attorney Edison, however, was angry. "Wait, Your Honor. I'm ready to present my statement on behalf of Pine Haven. I wish to be allowed to speak before recessing for the weekend."

"No, counselor. We'll start fresh on Monday."

"But Judge Lewis, what about the question of Teddy's custody during this hearing? We have a motion before the court stating Teddy should reside with Ralph, his rightful owner, at Pine Haven until his permanent residency is determined."

Arthur and I exchanged puzzled glances. We were never notified of any motion for temporary custody by Pine Haven.

"Your motion is granted Mr. Edison." Judge Lewis declared. Arthur sprang to his feet. "Your Honor, how can...."

"Relax, Mr. Jackson. There's nothing further to discuss. Until the court formally rules on this case, there is no legal reason to deprive Ralph Sullivan of his property."

Mark and Laura groaned.

Judge Lewis persisted. "The dog's ownership papers are in Ralph Sullivan's name. There's nothing I am prepared to do about that fact at this time."

"Thank you, Your Honor." Mr. Edison grinned.

Judge Lewis didn't appreciate his smugness. His voice raised a decibel or two. "That doesn't mean that I will order Teddy to stay with Ralph permanently." Mr. Edison looked down at the wooden floor.

"We will recess until nine o'clock Monday morning."

CHAPTER 12

Expecting the Unexpected

Arthur had asked me to give our summation. This was an honor, but one that scared me witless. I spent Saturday practicing in front of the mirror in another economy hotel room. Thirty-nine dollars a night. Another night Moriah and I would share pizza in the room; she knew she might even get a bite.

I pretended Jolene was critiquing me and began to practice aloud one more time.

"Your Honor, we are ready to prove that Teddy not only wants to continue to live with the Sullivans, but also that it is in his best interests to do so. Our observations demonstrate that Teddy is happy with the Sullivans. In fact he clearly appears uncertain and unhappy during visits to Pine Haven Home, even declining food altogether."

The phone rang. There were only two people who knew my hotel number. Hearing from either of them would not be good news.

"Hello, Carolyn?" It was Helena. My body stiffened. "She's gone, Carolyn."

Even though I knew the first day that I walked into her room that she was dying, I was stunned.

"She asked me to call you after she died and give you a message." She paused. "Are you there, Carolyn?"

"I'm here."

"She said to keep doing what you're doing. Give it everything you have." Then after a pause, she finished, "Tell her not to forget we've got feelings, too. Does that mean anything to you?"

"It does."

Helena's voice quivered. "Was she talking about your feelings or hers or one of the animals?"

"All of that."

There was a long silence. Helena wanted more. I willed my brain to think.

"We had some gut-wrenching conversations. We both get—got—torn up about animals suffering; so many in need of help. If animals could, they'd say 'We've got feelings too'. And the law doesn't care. But…"

I paused. Here was the real lesson. Helena waited. "But, not at the expense of ignoring our own. That's why she said that. She was reminding me." I didn't know what more I could tell her.

"Jo wanted you to take Mariah. Would you be willing to adopt her?"

"Sure. I'd be honored. Thank you, Helena."

"Thank you Carolyn, for telling her how much her work mattered. It gave her comfort to know that you are going forward. Best of luck to you."

That was it. Jolene was gone.

At that moment, half of me wanted to spend the next six months in bed in tears. The other half wanted to take Jo's baton and finish the race. This is the half I sided with.

I had to. For them.

I continued to rehearse, but on auto-pilot.

"It is true that Teddy might be able to get used to a new home given enough time. However, the question is not whether Teddy *is able* to get used to Pine Haven Home, but whether he *wants* to." My voice died out. My head was spinning.

I quit and went to bed.

Again the phone clanged. The only other person who had my number here was my brother. I reached over and picked it up and heard sobbing.

"What's wrong?"

"Mom has cancer again. It's her pancreas this time. She's decided not to have any treatment."

Spirit, Jolene, Mom.

That was it. My dingy hotel-room-world blurred then shattered.

I couldn't even think about getting up.

CHAPTER 13

A Modern *Lassie-Come-Home* Miracle

Moriah saved me. I was forced to get out of bed to take her for her walk. Watching my little tri-color dog lifted my spirits as she always does. I wondered how she would adopt to a new sibling. Obviously one of them would need a nickname. We could pick up Mariah on our way back to Vermont…whenever that would be. Our work here would soon be over one way or another. But what about my mother?

Monday morning Judge Lewis strode into his chambers and wasted no time. "It has come to my attention that Teddy ran away from Ralph and Pine Haven Home on Saturday night. Has the dog been recovered?"

"Yes, Your Honor," Mark Sullivan offered. "Teddy came home to my wife and me early yesterday morning."

"Judge, I wonder if the dog ran away or was he taken? The Sullivans live three dozen miles away from Pine Haven. That's a considerable distance for a dog to travel by himself, especially one his age." Mr. Edison's anger had dissolved over the weekend to desperation. A good sign.

"Are you suggesting we kidnapped Ted? That we stole our own dog?" It was Mark Sullivan's turn to be mad. He had history with this dog that was full of courage and companionship. "Are you?"

Judge Lewis wasn't interested in theatrics. "Excuse me gentlemen. This *is* a legal proceeding. Let's continue to observe the appropriate decorum."

"Your Honor, if the court will note. This is not the first time Teddy has run away from the Home," Arthur interjected. "He's done it twice before during scheduled visits with Ralph. Each time he found his way back to the Sullivans."

"That's right, Judge. We don't need an expert to tell us what that means! Ted wants to live with us." Mark wanted Ted back as quickly as possible.

"Where is Teddy right now?"

"He is at our home, Your Honor," Laura Sullivan responded.

"Alright. I've heard everything I need to hear. I'm ready to give you my decision. Everyone take your seats."

This was an astounding development. Could it be…?

"But Your Honor, I haven't had a chance to formally present a statement for my client, Pine Haven." Mr. Edison remained standing.

"You've done plenty of talking Mr. Edison. I have heard enough." On afterthought Judge Lewis added, "And seen enough. Please sit."

"Your Honor, Teddy *does* enjoy being a therapy dog at Pine Haven," Mr. Edison whined. "He might act a little shy, but the boys love him. Pine Haven needs him for their program. We want to show that

Teddy is very attached to Ralph. Living there, he clearly benefits a high percentage of the boys. Even allowing the use of *Teddy's Test*, the third prong provides Your Honor the option of considering 'the greater good of society'. Surely the mental development of a home full of needy boys is more important to society than the happiness of one old dog. I therefore request that you place Teddy permanently in Pine Haven Home."

"I understand counselor, thank you. Now take your seat."

Mr. Edison reluctantly straightened his chair and sat.

"I also understand that Teddy belongs to Ralph, papers and all. However, he clearly is a sentient being that has feelings for the people who have cared for him all of his life. Therefore, no guardian *ad litem* appointment is necessary. The dog, himself, has demonstrated an unmistakable desire to reside with the Sullivans."

"I am finding Teddy, this collie dog, to be sentient or feeling property. Living with his legal owner Ralph Sullivan, would cause the dog undue emotional distress. It is unreasonable for Pine Haven Home to presume the right to use the dog for therapy just because the dog's owner is a resident. I am, however, ordering Teddy be taken to Pine Haven Home for bi-monthly supervised visitations. You've got your precedent, Mr. Jackson. Use it wisely."

Bang! That was it.

"Thank you, Judge Lewis." Arthur jammed his files into his briefcase, as if he needed to get out of the room before the judge changed his mind.

Sentient property precedent. We had it! Better yet, it was Teddy himself who proved his own case. He was a *Lassie Come Home* miracle all over again. If I'd planned for years, I could not have dreamed such a perfect ending.

CHAPTER 14

Closeness and Closure

Teddy's and Spirit's cases leapt across the headlines the same week.

PET'S DEATH CLASSIFIED AS LOST BAGGAGE

MODERN APPROACH TO ANIMAL LAW UNLEASHED IN COURT

The New York court went on to allow Adam and his new lawyer to amend their complaint. They stated a new cause of action for fraud against the airline and demanded a million dollars in damages. But the case never went to a jury. Instead, the attorney settled out of court for fifteen thousand dollars. At the time, 1995, it was the largest amount ever awarded for the death of a companion animal.

Spirit and Jolene left us a legacy. Their case has been used in legal circles ever since as a classic example of the need to update our legal system.

Jolene died thinking she had lost. She was wrong.

Without legal action, Spirit's life would have meant nothing to East West Airlines who would not have blinked at paying out the maximum twelve hundred fifty dollars for lost 'baggage'. By getting the case into court, Ms. Marion forced the airline to pay attention to Spirit's death and rewrite its policies on animal transportation. Other airlines have followed suit.

Jolene forced the legal system to begin looking at its outdated common law regarding animals. Her tenacity helped lay the foundation for Teddy's case.

The American Transportation Association states that more than five hundred thousand animals are transported by air every year. An estimated five thousand are killed, injured or lost each year due to extreme heat or cold, or mishandling by baggage personnel. Jolene would have been especially pleased when then President William Clinton signed the Safe Air Travel for Animals Act on April 5, 2000, five years following her death.

It was time to leave Kalamazoo and drive home to see my mother. To my amazement, she'd asked when I was coming. That was as close as she would come to saying she needed help. Now I knew why she'd sounded distant. She didn't want me to worry about her in the middle of Teddy's case.

When I arrived, she was weak and in bed. Her skin was grayish. She handed me a newspaper article. It was about our case. She whispered, "I've been following your case Sweetie." I leaned forward gripping the only chair to steady myself. She hadn't called me 'Sweetie'…in how long? "You're strong, Carolyn. You've loved animals your whole life. Keep following your heart." It was a wonderful, welcome affirmation.

The effort exhausted her. Her eyes remained closed. The end was coming. Now it was my turn to be the helper.

Tick, Tick. Quick, quick.

I marveled that she had asked *me* to be with her. Me, the one she didn't like. My heart thumped so heavily, I thought it might quit. How does one do this? I was determined to do whatever it took.

Only a month ago she was playing 'fish faces' with her great grandchildren. She'd looked so pretty and tastefully dressed. I remembered how suddenly the realization hit; she was so thin she had to keep hoisting up her pants. It must have taken that army general in her to pull off that last playful goodbye for the sake of her children.

Looking at her now, the memory brought up a love for her so fierce, I ached.

At eighty-four, she was done fighting. No more surgery this time. She wanted me to be there for my father and, I think, help her stay free of pain. She'd made every preparation a human being could make for her death—from giving her slides of Greece to a Greek Architecture graduate student to planning her post-funeral-party she named 'The Whoop-Dee-Do.' Still, I sat wondering how a person did anything like this. How do you *do* death?

Her end room in the single-level assisted living building was so quiet. I thought of Helena and Jolene. This time, I was the one in the room next to the bed wondering if I should read to her or play music or just sit and be with her.

What did she need? What was I supposed to do? Where were the instructions? She liked to listen to town politics over the local radio station. Now she was too weak to turn it on and didn't want to listen.

Memories and more memories swamped my thoughts. I saw my life with her so differently. What an honor to be the daughter and advocate for this brave, independent woman who had taken me canoeing before I could walk; who had shown me through her example that it was alright to take my own path in life.

She no longer seemed able to communicate accept for eye blinks—one for 'yes', two for 'no'. "Mom, are you in pain?" Two blinks.

Or maybe she didn't want to be in touch. Perhaps she was going through her own private preparation for death as the Hospice booklet suggested.

I'd watched Jolene's caregivers. How was it done? The answer came, "Each in your own way. There *is* no one right way."

Weeks passed and with them challenges I hoped I'd never face. A nurse asked me if there was anything she was holding onto. I thought, honestly, that there could be lots of things. Maybe it would be a good idea to talk with her one more time—just in case I could help her let go. I knew it would be tough.

Sobbing, I held Mom's hand in both of mine and thanked her for everything she had given me and done for me—everything I could think of—from the very beginning to this present moment. I hoped she could hear me.

When I finished, the room was silent. I knew she was not one to show feelings, so on second thought I added, "I'm probably making you really uncomfortable with all this blubbering. Sorry."

Was that a faint pressure on my fingers? Was it? Had she heard? Very slowly my mother turned her face toward me, her eyes still tightly closed. Her face softened. She squeezed my hand for the second time!

A rush of joy.

We did a good death.

CHAPTER 15

Your Turn

Tears can be healing...and the wounded are everywhere. Often people say, "I just heard the most awful thing on the news." Animal lovers, faces ridden with angst and disgust, tell me about the latest animal story they've heard or read. "It's terrible," they lament.

We have all heard them.

A surprising number go on to say, "If there is anything I can do to help you, I'll do it."

Now there is. How?

The next time you hear about such a case, here are several suggestions that will take little time or money at all:

- Call information and get the telephone number of the television station or newspaper reporting the story. Ask to speak to the reporter who reported it, whether local or national. If you can't speak to a reporter directly, leave a message. Thank them for their report. Tell them that you know about a new way to handle animal cases by using a new legal principle called *sentient*, or *feeling*, property.

- Ask for the reporter's address or email and send them a letter or press release about a new legal way to handle animal cases. Email a press release to a friend or business person. You can find one online at www.WeveGotFeelingsToo.com, click on the 'In the Media' link and click on "Email sentient property summary."
- Write a letter or email of support to the lawyer taking an animal case and copy the judge(s).
- If you are an attorney, use the term 'sentient property' in your brief. *Petco v. Schuster*, a Texas case, first introduced sentient property in Footnote #6, April 29, 2004. Share your experiences at info@animallegalreports.com.
- If you are a judge, use the term 'sentient or feeling property' in your opinion.
- If you are a veterinarian, you want all your clients to have a strong bond with their pets. Be a hero instead of an ostrich. Acknowledge and encourage clients to talk about their relationship with their nonhuman family members and work with the use of sentient property as it is used in courts or legislation. Note that in states where MD's have med-mal caps (~19), insurance rates are more likely to be above the national median. Other factors are driving up physician insurance premiums.[1] You are a group admired by so many, including this author. No one wants you to pay the fees MDs do for your malpractice insurance. It is unrealistic to simply oppose *any*

---

[1] Weiss Ratings: Medical Malpractice Caps, *The Impact of Non-Economic Damage Caps on Physician Premiums, Claims, Payout Levels, and Availability of Coverage*, June 2, 2003.

heightened legal status for animals. Learn what to do in your state while you can make a difference.
- If you are a politician or a legislator, use the term 'sentient or feeling property' as you draft local and state ordinances.
- Internationally, if you hear of or are a lawyer taking an animal case, encourage them to mail or email *Animal Legal Reports Services* at the Web site above. Case stories may be chosen as chapters in the next book. We all know the world is getting smaller. Let's share the news about what we are legally doing for animals worldwide.

In short, offer sentient property information to animal lovers, lawyers and judges, to your tennis partners and golf cronies, church members, corporate management, garden clubs, neighbors and co-workers; to book clubs, humane societies, environmental organizations, teachers, and libraries.

You or someone you know may bring the first precedent-setting sentient property case to court.

Life does get in the way, but if you agree that our legal system needs to catch up with times and show greater respect and compassion for animals, honor them by raising their property status to sentient property.

Today is a good day to succeed.

Epilogue

Jolene's grave pictured below with the author's dogs:

Kenya   **Teddy**

The headstone reads:

> Jolene Ruth Marion
> April 21, 1941 – May 22, 1994
> Loving Wife
> Beloved Sister
> Esteemed Friend
> Dedicated Her Life to Alleviate Animal Suffering

The dogwood is a symbol of martyrdom. The lion is lying down with the lamb.

Three years after her death on a rainy, dark and billowy day, I drove slowly through a Long Island cemetery in search of her grave. I thought she wouldn't mind my dogs paying her a visit with me. She'd probably think it was great fun to have them there.

Loving Wife.

I learned Michael, her former husband, had supported Jolene through twenty-two years of a marriage that crescendoed into turbulent times over heartbreaking animal cases and continuous care for their many cats and dogs. Although they divorced four years prior to her illness and death, Michael paid the bill for Jolene's funeral expenses. When I got the chance to meet him, I was not surprised by his generosity. He seemed to really care. Somehow that made standing in front of her grave even more meaningful.

I murmured "Hello" and proceeded to share some thoughts with any Spirit or spirits that might be hanging around in the gray drizzle of the afternoon. Following a quiet time, we left. I felt somehow I had received permission to memorialize this woman who, according to Helena, was both a martyr and a saint.

To me, Spirit and Jolene were both martyrs. Theirs was a symbiotic life-and-death relationship. Through Spirit, Jolene's life took on greater consequence; through Jolene, Spirit's life was immortalized. Their legacies continue as one in this book.

May 24, 1994

Jolene R. Marion
Lawyer, 53

Jolene R. Marion, a New York lawyer who played a prominent role in the animal rights movement, died on Sunday at the Queens home of a friend. She was 53 and lived in Manhattan.

The cause was breast cancer, her family said.

At her death, she was an adjunct professor at the Pace University School of Law. She also continued to represent clients.

A native of Brooklyn, Ms. Marion began her animal-rescue work while an undergraduate at Queens College in 1970. She graduated from Seton Hall Law School in 1976 and became an insistent voice among advocates of animal-rights laws to ban leghold traps and other cruel practices.

She was associated with a number of other organizations, including the Animal Legal Defense Fund and Legal Action for Animals. Much of her work was pro bono, with clients ranging from individual pet owners to humane organizations.

She is survived by her sister, Helena of Long Island.

Copyright © 1994 by The New York Times Co. Reprinted with permission.